SKILLS FOR LIFE

SKILLS FOR LIFE

Lesley Kaye-Besley
N.E. Surrey College of Technology

Dilwyn Byles
Merthyr Tydfil Technical College

STUDENT'S EDITION
REVISED AND UPDATED

General Editor:

Ray Taylor, Principal of Merthyr Tydfil Technical College

Stanley Thornes (Publishers) Ltd.

First published in 1979 by:
Stanley Thornes (Publishers) Ltd.
Educa House
Old Station Drive
Leckhampton
CHELTENHAM GL53 0DN
England

Reprinted 1980
Reprinted 1981
Reprinted with minor amendments 1983
Revised and updated 1984

British Library Cataloguing in Publication Data
Kaye-Besley, Lesley
    Skills for life.—Student's ed. revised and updated
    1. Great Britain—Social conditions—1945 –
    I. Title   II. Byles, Dilwyn   III. Taylor, R.J.
    941.058'8   HN 385.5

    ISBN 0 85950 204 X

Typesetting by Artmark Nailsworth, Gloucestershire
Printed in Great Britain at The Pitman Press, Bath

Tutor's Preface

Skills for Life has been produced out of a growing demand for a text to meet the needs of young people who are about to make, or who have just made, the transition from school to the 'world outside'. *Skills for Life* is an attempt to provide both tutor and student with a sourcebook which will develop interest and enthusiasm at work, at home and at leisure.

Skills for Life has been stimulated by the provision of social and life skills courses in schools, colleges, voluntary institutions and not the least in the YOP and now the Youth Training Scheme.

As the Manpower Services Commission has said, 'Many people lack some of the basic day-to-day skills which most of us take for granted. Social and Life Skills refer to all those abilities, bits of information, know-how and decision making which we all need in order to get by in life.' The transition to the world of work throws up countless problems for young people, but if they are shielded by self-discipline and self-motivation, and armed with a variety of skills and experiences, the transition becomes far less painful. *Skills for Life* attempts to bring students into confrontation with all sorts of situations and help them to meet those situations with equanimity and indeed confidence.

It is very necessary to be realistic with relation to the employment situation for young people once their school, college or Youth Training Scheme is over. After all, it is quite possible that, with the increased automation of the 'Silicon Chip Age', the days when 95 per cent of us will work at one job for 40-odd years are over. Already we are into the era of frequent retraining and early retirement for many people, and it is easy to envisage a time when more and more of us will never work, in the accepted sense of the word, only because there is no work for us to do.

Michael Kaye-Besley, former Head of General Studies at Merthyr Tydfil Technical College, wrote in a Foreword to the first printing of this book: "The basis of Aldous Huxley's *Brave New World* lies in the theory that 'the nuclear scientist will prepare a bed on which mankind must lie; and if mankind doesn't fit, well, that is just too bad for mankind'. This is standardisation of the human product taken to its extreme, and yet the philosophy continues to creep into our education system and our society. Now is the time to fight this standardisation, and perhaps social and life skills courses, such as outlined in *Skills for Life*, provide us with an opportunity to begin this fight."

Contents

Chapter 1

Community Services

Using Local Agencies

Do you know where to go for help when you have a problem? Life is very complicated today. We have a different organisation for every aspect of our life. If you have a local Citizens Advice Bureau, you are very fortunate, because they can always help.

Fill in the questionnaire on the next page and keep it carefully so that you will be able to look up the answer when you next need a problem solved.

WHERE WOULD YOU GO FOR THE FOLLOWING?

1. To find out the names of local councillors _____
2. To find out the name of your MP _____
3. To find out the owner of a piece of land _____
4. To find out about buying a house _____
5. To find out about evening classes _____
6. To book theatre tickets _____
7. To have jewellery valued _____
8. To join the TAVR _____
9. To have a carpet cleaned _____
10. To MOT test your car _____
11. To get hold of an unusual book _____
12. To register the birth of a baby _____
13. To find out about local residents' associations _____
14. To arrange a wedding _____
15. To put an advert in the newspaper _____
16. To find out about the history of your home town _____
17. To see your MP _____
18. To get a pregnancy test _____
19. To complain about your child's education _____
20. To get hold of a doctor on a Sunday _____
21. To complain about refuse collection _____
22. To get your money back on faulty goods when the shop concerned will not help _____
23. To query your income tax _____
24. To apply for a driving test _____
25. To obtain Family Income Supplement _____
26. To collect an Old Age Pension _____
27. To collect OAP cheap travel cards _____
28. To get a washing machine fixed _____
29. To find out about legal aid _____
30. To pay your rates _____
31. To look for a new job _____
32. To get a prescription on a Sunday _____
33. To register as unemployed _____
34. To change your surname _____
35. To buy a road vehicle licence _____

36. To find out a telephone number in another town _____
37. To buy a television licence _____
38. To insure a house against fire and theft _____
39. To report faults in a council house _____
40. To apply for a passport _____
41. To report blocked drains _____
42. To put your house up for sale _____
43. To call the fire brigade _____
44. To get help for unfair dismissal _____
45. To get a solicitor to act for you _____
46. To know what has gone on in a Council Meeting _____
47. To find out how long a power cut is going to last _____
48. To find out about your civil rights _____
49. To see a specialist doctor at the hospital _____
50. To ask for any sort of help or advice _____

How do we get the dole?
Where's the hospital?
Can I get a council house?

How do we get married?
Can I travel cheaply
Can I see my MP?

He's left me. How am I going to manage?

Communicating

How good are you at selling yourself? Do you come away from meeting others fed up with yourself for the things you said, and the things you didn't manage to say?

We are going to look at this aspect of ourselves in this unit. You will find a mock application form opposite. Can you fill it in, in such a way that the person reading it will get a good impression of you? When you have finished, swap forms with the person sitting beside you and see if you would give him/her a job!

On page 8 you will find a cartoon of Fred. How would you sum up his problem? Would you give him the job?

The Scottish poet Robert Burns wrote:

> *O wad some Pow'r the giftie gie us*
> *To see oursels as others see us!!*

—do you agree?

Application Form for a College Place on a Social and Life Skills Course

State

Your name (surname first) _____

Your address _____

_____

Your age in years and months _____

Your last school _____

Your hobbies and interests _____

_____

_____

The job you would most like to do if you could choose _____

_____

_____

The wages you think you are worth _____

Things about yourself which would be useful to an employer _____

_____

_____

The names and addresses of two people who will give you a reference

1) _____

_____

2) _____

_____

Your reasons for applying for this college course _____

_____

_____

_____

Introducing Social Security

Most people would agree that Social Security in this country is complicated. Perhaps you have already had to deal with some aspect of it, and have discovered that for yourself.

In Unit 1.3 we are going to have a look at some of the different kinds of help offered by the Department of Health and Social Security. We are also going to look at how you apply for sick pay, because most people need to do this sooner or later.

Department of Health & Social Security (DHSS)

In our society we attempt to make sure that no one goes hungry, cold, sick or neglected. Everyone who is in a position to do so, pays contributions into a 'general pool', and that money is used to benefit those who need it. At some time in his or her life, almost everyone pays into and draws from this 'pool'. The 'pool' pays for our 'free' Health Service.

At present everyone starts to pay a National Insurance contribution once more than a few pounds per week have been earned. Once this contribution has been paid for approximately 18 months one is entitled to claim:

Unemployment Benefit
Sickness Benefit (if you are not getting SSP—see page 12)
Disablement Benefit
Invalidity Benefit
Maternity Benefit
Retirement Benefit (Pension)
Widow's Benefit
Widowed Mother's Benefit

All these are *contributory* benefits–but society also looks after the people who, for various reasons, have not been able to pay into the 'pool'. These *non-contributory* benefits are called **Supplementary Benefits**. How much money the individual is given each week depends on his or her circumstances and needs. The Social Security Office assesses each case individually. Supplementary Benefits include:

Youth Unemployment Benefit (for school leavers who cannot find work)

Family Income Supplement (for families who do not have enough to live on)

Attendance Allowance (for looking after the sick and elderly)

Mobility Allowance (to help the handicapped get around)

Rent and Rate Rebates (for those who cannot afford their homes)

Finally, there are **Exceptional Circumstance Additions**, which can be paid to anyone who can prove real need. Again, they are *assessed* by the local DHSS. They can be given for almost any need, but the most common are:

Special Diets

Laundry

Heavy wear and tear on clothes because of disability

Hire-purchase for essentials (less common)

Help for a woman who has left work to look after sick or aged relatives

Fares for regular visits to relative in hospital or prison

Child-minding costs

If you are ill

You are normally entitled to Statutory Sick Pay (SSP) if you are away from work because of illness (though there are some restrictions for *short* periods of illness). Nowadays you do not need a note from a doctor unless your illness lasts more than seven days (this includes a weekend; it doesn't mean seven *working* days).

If you are away from work for less than seven days, however, you do need to fill in a 'Self-Certification of Sickness' form; the exact layout of this varies from employer to employer, but a typical example (slightly less than the real size) is shown on page 13. You can get blank forms from your employer. Take a careful look at the form, and if possible practise filling one in. Almost everyone will have to do this at some time; in fact many employers ask you to fill in a copy of the form if you are away ill even for *one* day.

As the form says, 'any entitlement to Statutory Sick Pay will depend on the evidence of sickness you provide' on the form, so it is quite important to fill it in correctly! You pass the completed form to your employer.

If you are away ill for more than a week, you do still need a 'doctor's statement', which supports your claim for sick pay. You get your doctor to fill in the statement form, and pass it to your employer.

Normally your employer gives you the sick pay, just like your normal pay. However, in certain circumstances the SSP stops, and you get Sickness Benefit from the DHSS. (The most usual reason is that an employee has already received eight weeks' SSP from the employer during that tax year.)

You may never need to know how to apply to the DHSS for this; but if you do, your employer at the time should know how to do it.

One final important point: you should let your employer know *immediately* that you are ill when you begin any period of sick leave (even a day); otherwise the employer might refuse to consider it as time counting towards sick pay.

SELF-CERTIFICATION
of SICKNESS

Employer

PLEASE READ THESE NOTES CAREFULLY. IF THERE IS ANYTHING YOU DO NOT UNDERSTAND, ASK YOUR SUPERVISOR.

As soon as you return to work after a sickness absence of 7 days or less, you must complete this Self-Certification form.
Any entitlement to Statutory Sick Pay will depend on the evidence of sickness you provide below.

   a) Complete this form in your supervisor's presence, using BLOCK CAPITALS.
   b) The 'Period of Sickness' dates must be the first and last days of your ACTUAL SICKNESS, even if these occurred on rest days, Public Holidays, or other days you would not normally work.
   c) Certify your reason for absence, then sign and date the form; your supervisor will then countersign it as witness to your signature.

Note: If your sickness exceeds 7 calendar days, ask your Doctor for a Medical Certificate as evidence that you were unfit for work.

Job Title / Department / Section	Number	Date of Birth			Forename(s)	Surname
		Day	Month	Year.		Mr. Mrs. Miss

I CERTIFY THAT I WAS UNFIT FOR WORK BECAUSE OF

	Put X in correct box
ILLNESS	**X**
EMPLOYMENT ACCIDENT	
OTHER ACCIDENT	

PERIOD OF SICKNESS Enter 1st and last dates of sickness even if not normal working days	From	Time	Day	Date		To	Time	Day	Date
		am/pm		/ /19			am/pm		/ /19

Did you become sick whilst at work? | If YES did you do any work that day?

PERIOD OF ABSENCE Enter dates absent from work	From	Time	Day	Date		To	Time	Day	Date
		am/pm		/ /19			am/pm		/ /19

Give **SYMPTOMS** of illness, or describe accident and cause

TREATMENT   Did you see a Doctor or visit a Hospital?   Please enter   YES or NO

If YES give name and address of Doctor or Hospital and state treatment	If NO describe any treatment or medicine you took to help your recovery

SSP/STATE BENEFITS	Has the DHSS given you an explanatory letter headed Statutory Sick Pay? i.e. Form ref. BF220, BF218, BM7 or BM8 (state YES/NO)	If YES, please hand the letter to your Supervisor

EMPLOYEE'S SIGNATURE		**SUPERVISOR'S SIGNATURE**	
I certify that the above is a true & correct record of my sickness and absence and understand that further enquiries may be made at the discretion of management	Date	The above details were completed and signed in my presence	Date

NOTES   Office use only   If an Employment Accident has been certified above, check the Notification of Accidents and Dangerous Occurrence Regulations.

SSP DETAILS	Nat. Ins. Number		Is evidence of incapacity acceptable?	
No. of days Sickness	Date Notified			
No. of days Qualifying	How Notified		If NO, give reasons	
SSP/State Benefit Linking	Attach DHSS form BF220, BF218, BM7 or BM8 if provided by employee	DHSS form ref.		
		Last date of SSP Exclusion		

COPY FOR

FS.141
R.1
Reproduction of this form, in whole or in part, requires written consent from the Publishers and Suppliers   FORMECON SERVICES LTD., 1983
FORMECON SERVICES LTD., DOUGLAS HOUSE, GATEWAY, CREWE, CW1 1YN   Telephone 0270 587311   Telex 36550

Introducing the Law

Do you know anything about the law of our land? What rights have you got? What rights has a policeman got? Why are there so many different kinds of Court?

In Unit 1.4 we are going to have a quick look at just two aspects of Law: the way it affects young people, and the way the different Courts work. You will find that a useful source for some of this information is the Citizens Advice Bureau.

UNDER 18—YOU AND THE LAW

  A *School*

    1. Can parents choose which school their child attends? _____

    2. Are pupils automatically entitled to school milk? _____

    3. Can a teacher keep a child in after school? _____

    4. Can a school insist upon school uniform being worn? _____

    5. Whom does the law hold responsible if a child truants from school? _____

    6. At what age can children be expelled from school? _____

  B *Sickness and Health*

    1. At 15 years do you need parental consent for medical treatment? __ _____

    What about at 16 years? _____

    2. How old must you be to arrange to donate your kidneys or eyes or heart for transplant? _____

    3. At what age do you start paying towards the cost of your prescriptions? _____

    4. Can a 16-year-old donate blood? _____

    5. Is it possible to legally obtain cannabis, heroin and LSD? _____

    6. At what age can you get confidential contraceptive advice without parental knowledge? _____

    7. Can a 15-year-old have an abortion without parental permission? _____

    What about at 16 years? _____

    8. At what age may a girl legally consent to sexual intercourse? _____

    9. At what age can a boy be charged with rape? _____

    10. What are the two conditions for legal homosexual acts? _____

  C *Work and Money*

    1. At what age may children be employed? (The exceptions to this are appearing on the stage and helping parents with light agricultural work or a street market stall.) _____

2. At what age can people work in a pub? _____

3. At what age can youngsters join the Services?
   Boys _____

   Girls _____

4. At what age does your income belong to you? _____

5. Who can claim unemployment benefit? _____

6. Who can claim supplementary benefit? _____

7. How old do you have to be to open a bank account? _____

8. Can someone under 18 be sued for breach of contract? _____

D *The Police*
   1. Can the police search you without arresting you? _____

   2. Do the police need a warrant to search a building? _____

   3. At what age can you be arrested? _____

   4. At what age may the police take your fingerprints without parental permission? _____

   5. For how long can the police detain a young person? _____

   6. Are your fingerprints kept? _____

E *At Home*
   1. At what age does parental authority cease? _____

   2. Who chooses the religion of a child? _____

   3. At what age can you marry *with* parental consent? _____

   4. At what age can you marry *without* parental consent? _____

   5. Up to what age can you be adopted? _____

   6. How old must you be to adopt a child? _____

   7. Who places a child for adoption? _____

   8. What does 'illegitimate' mean? _____

   9. What surname does an illegitimate baby take? _____

10. At what age can you vote? _____

11. At what age can you obtain a passport? _____

12. At what age can you leave home? _____

F *Restrictive Activities*
1. At what age can you gamble? _____
2. At what age can you go into a pub? _____
3. At what age can you drink lemonade in a pub? _____
4. At what age can you drink beer and cider *with a meal* in a pub? _____
5. At what age can you drink what you choose in a pub? _____
6. How old do you have to be to drive a moped, _____

   a motorcycle, _____ a car? _____
7. At what age can you own a gun? _____
8. At what age can you buy fireworks? _____
9. At what age can you smoke cigarettes in your own home? _____
10. At what age can you be tattooed? _____

The Laws of England and Wales

The Courts

All proceedings in a Court of Law are called cases. The cases which come before the courts are either **criminal** or **civil**.

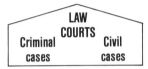

In **criminal** cases the court has to decide whether the accused person has broken the *law* of the land. If he is found guilty, he will be either:

i) fined, or
ii) imprisoned, or
iii) put on probation, or
iv) given a suspended sentence.

In **civil** cases the court has to settle an argument or a dispute between two people, and decide who should pay whom money. This money is called **damages**. There is no question of punishment.

Criminal Courts

Anyone who is charged with a crime is brought first before the **Magistrates' Court**. There is no jury in this court, just magistrates who hear the evidence and make a decision. In most places the magistrates are Justices of the Peace (JPs)—ordinary members of the community (not necessarily lawyers) who are not paid, though they can claim for expenses and loss of earnings. They deal with all the less serious crimes and can send a person to prison for up to six months, or fine him up to £1,000.

Juvenile Courts are special Magistrates' Courts for dealing with children who have broken the law.

If the crime is a more serious one, then the case will go on to the **Crown Court** for trial by a judge and jury. When the Crown Court sits in London it is known as the Central Criminal Court or **The Old Bailey.**

If the person who has been found guilty at either of these courts feels he has been treated unfairly, then he may ask a higher court to look at the case again. This is called an **Appeal**. The highest court in the land is the **House of Lords**.

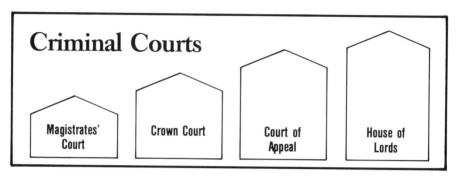

Criminal Courts

Magistrates' Court   Crown Court   Court of Appeal   House of Lords

Civil Courts

The **County Courts** were established in 1846, mainly in order to help people get back the small sums of money they were owed.

In a County Court there is usually one judge but *no* jury. The most common cases dealt with in a County Court are:

i) disputes between landlord and tenant

ii) personal injuries (where less than £5,000 is claimed)

iii) nuisances

iv) hire-purchase agreements

v) divorce cases (uncontested)

Where less than £500 is being claimed, there are special procedures to make it easy for people to present a case themselves without legal representation. Indeed, in many cases such claims are referred to an 'arbitrator' rather than a judge, and the proceedings are kept very simple. The atmosphere in an arbitration tends to be more informal than that of a court, and the evidence is heard in private, whereas members of the public are entitled to attend a trial.

More serious cases go to the **High Court**, as do all divorce cases where one partner does not wish for the divorce. As with criminal cases, it is possible to appeal against the decision of the court. From the County Court, one appeals to the Court of Appeal and from there to the House of Lords.

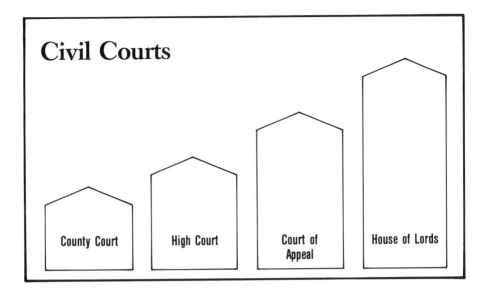

Other Tribunals

Twenty years ago it was decided to set up special courts where a lot of technical knowledge about the subjects was necessary. These special courts are also called **Tribunals** and include:

   i) Agricultural Land

  ii) Rent

 iii) National Insurance

 iv) National Health Service

  v) Pensions Appeal

 vi) Industrial

Anyone who is unhappy with the decision of the Tribunal may appeal to the High Court.

Coroners' Court

It is the job of the Coroner to decide why a person has died when the dead person's doctor is not absolutely certain that the death was natural. The case before a Coroners' Court is called an inquest.

UNIT
1.5

Introducing Income Tax

In Unit 1.5 we are going on to have a look at how income tax affects our lives, for these days it is the basis of our country's economy. Income tax affects us all. Even if you don't pay it, you almost certainly soon will, and other members of your family are paying it at this very minute. Nobody likes paying income tax, so why do we go on paying it?

You will need a copy of Inland Revenue leaflet IR2 to be able to answer the questions. The Inland Revenue are the people who collect the income tax for the government.

Income tax is a direct tax upon the money you earn. How much tax you pay depends on:

i) How much you earn
ii) Whether or not you have any savings making money for you
iii) How many people are dependent upon you
iv) The rate of tax fixed by the Chancellor of the Exchequer in his budget

Income tax was introduced by William Pitt in 1799 to finance the war against France. Everyone so hated it that in 1816, when the war was over, it was abolished.

However, it was reintroduced in 1842 by Robert Peel, and it has been levied ever since. Now it is the most important part of government finance. The money they collect from us is used for building main roads and motorways, supporting education, the Health Service, new government buildings and a thousand other expenses for our benefit.

Most countries of the world have some form of income tax, and these days all regard it as a 'necessary evil'. Perhaps the best consolation comes from Rudyard Kipling who said:

Whoever pays the taxes, owns the land.

What do you think this means?

How much do you know about income tax? Try doing the exercise over the page.

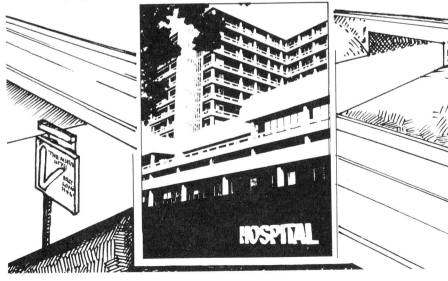

1. What are the dates of the tax year? _____

2. What is the personal allowance for:
a single person? _____

a married man with wife not taxed separately? _____

3. What is the basic rate of income tax? _____

4. At what age do you start paying income tax? _____

5. What does PAYE mean? _____

6. How often in the year do we pay income tax? _____

7. Who tells your employer how much tax to take out of your wage packet? _____

8. What is meant by a tax code? _____

9. Do you get a tax code on your first day at work? _____

10. How do you get a form to claim tax allowances? _____

11. Does every working person fill in an Income Tax Return form? ____

12. How do you find out what allowances you can claim? _____

13. Do you get tax relief for your National Insurance contribution?____

14. Can I claim tax relief for the cost of my tools to do my job? _____

15. What is a P45? _____

16. If you are given an emergency tax code while a new code is being sorted out, do you get the excess tax back? _____

17. Do you pay income tax when you are unemployed?_____

18. How much can you earn a week before you pay income tax? _____

19. Do you pay tax on money earned in a spare-time job? _____

20. Do you pay tax on unearned income? _____

What is Insurance?

Which companies have insurance offices in the High Street of your local town, and what do they do behind those shiny plate-glass windows? Have you ever plucked up courage to go in and find out for yourself?

In Unit 1.6 we are going to take a quick look at the basics of insurance, as it affects most ordinary people. If you go into a couple of your local insurance offices, they will almost certainly give you some of their attractive booklets to add to your work in the group.

At some time in our lives we all **need** insurance of some kind. There are many kinds of insurance and many different Insurance Companies. Insurance is called **cover** because your needs are protected or covered if something happens to you. There are two kinds of cover: **INSURANCE** and **ASSURANCE**.

Insurance is cover against something that **might** happen to you.

Assurance is cover against something that **will** happen to you.

So we take out insurance in case of fire in our home, an accident at work, a car accident or losing our luggage on holiday. We take out an assurance policy on our life. We are all going to die, so the money is assured on our death. (This money may pay for the funeral or help the people who are left behind to cope without us.) If an assurance policy is taken out for a certain length of time, then when that time is up, we are assured that the money will be paid out.

What insurance do you need?

There are some kinds of General Branch Insurance which you must have **by law**. These include:

i) Motor car insurance } (in case others are hurt)
ii) Motor bike insurance
iii) Employer's liability (in case of an accident at his works that is his fault)

There are other kinds of General Branch Insurance which it is **wise** to have. These include insurance for:

i) A house
ii) House contents
iii) Jewellery and valuables
iv) Business premises
v) Farm and farm animals

The sum you pay each year is call a **premium**. How big your premium is will depend on the value of the thing you wish to insure and how likely it is that the thing might be damaged or destroyed. At a price, it is possible to insure almost anything.

What about assurance?

Basically there are two kinds of Life Assurance: Whole Life Assurance and Endowment Assurance. Again the sum you pay each year is called the **premium**, and the number of years it is taken out for is called the **term**. The size of the premium will depend on the age of the person and how big an assurance policy he wishes to buy.

WHOLE LIFE ASSURANCE is paid out at death.

ENDOWMENT ASSURANCE is paid out either at death or at the end of the *term*, whichever comes *first*.

So, while insurance gives you peace of mind, but often nothing more, assurance is a **form of saving**.

e.g.

Fred is a young husband aged 25. He decides to take out an endowment assurance policy with a term of 30 years. This means when he is 55 he will get back a large sum of money (his savings plus interest). If he dies before he reaches 55, the company will give his widow and children money.

How do you pay for insurance and assurance policies?

This depends entirely on you, the company and the sort of insurance. The Insurance Agent or 'Clubman' may call at the door every week to collect the money and mark the book. Alternatively, it is possible to pay your premium once a year by cheque and never see the Insurance Agent.

What happens to the money paid in?

The money that is collected in is handled very carefully. Obviously large sums have to be kept where they can be got at quickly to pay out for claims and accidents. The bulk of the money is invested in big companies such as Marks & Spencer, ICI, Boots the Chemists and Allied Breweries. Therefore, the money helps other industries as well as earning interest.

Personal Budgeting

When you were quite small, did you have a few pennies of pocket money to spend? Did you rush out and spend the whole lot on sweets on a Saturday morning, or did you keep some for later in the week, or were you one of those goody-goody children who put it all in a piggy bank?

Whatever you chose to do with those few pennies, they were the beginnings of your elementary budgeting. These days, your finances are bound to be more complicated. Do you, for instance, make a contribution at home for your keep?

In Unit 1.7 this is the subject we are considering. In the first exercise you will have to do some arithmetic. On page 31, you are to make a decision on how much you think people should be paid. On page 32 we would like you to try to fill in all the prices, first by guessing, and then by going to look round the shops.

When the Chancellor of the Exchequer presents his budget to Parliament, he is giving an estimate of the **nation's** spending and buying for the coming year.

Family and personal budgeting should be exactly the same process on a much smaller scale, for in order to make the best of one's money, one should know how to manage it. At any level, the process is one of weighing alternatives and making choices within the limits of available money.

Many surveys have drawn the conclusion that the following table represents the approximate budget of many families:

Housing and getting to work	15%
Power supplies	10%
Food and drink	30%
Clothes and shoes	10%
Household expenses	15%
Luxuries and savings	20%
	100%

So if one applies these figures to some take-home pay packets, what is the result? Fill in the gaps in the table below.

TAKE HOME PAY:	£50	£75	£100	£125
Housing:	£	£	£	£
Power:	£	£	£	£
Food:	£	£	£	£
Clothes:	£	£	£	£
Household:	£	£	£	£
Extras:	£	£	£	£
TOTAL:	£	£	£	£

HOW MUCH SHOULD PEOPLE BE PAID?

Set out below are **ten** very different jobs. In each case the person doing the job is aged 40 years. Bearing in mind such factors as the amount of education and training necessary, the value of the work to the community and country, the danger involved in the work, the working hours, and the responsibility involved, you must decide how much each should earn. The minimum is £60 per week. The maximum is £600 per week. Write you answers in below, and be prepared to defend your decision.

	Your answer	Group answer
Solicitor	£	£
Miner	£	£
Member of Parliament	£	£
Social Worker	£	£
Secretary	£	£
Factory Manager	£	£
Teacher	£	£
Air Hostess	£	£
Factory Worker	£	£
Doctor	£	£

Date . . . .

Article	Estimated Price £ p	Actual Price £ p
large loaf of bread		
dozen no. 3 eggs		
pint of milk		
1 lb of Cheddar cheese		
5 lb of potatoes		
1 lb of minced beef		
250 g of butter		
$3\frac{1}{2}$ lb frozen chicken		
washing powder (size E3)		
100 g of instant coffee		
pack of 40 tea bags		
bottle of orange squash		
1 lb box of chocolates		
200 g of chocolate biscuits		
washing up liquid (540 ml)		
1 lb (454 g) jar of raspberry jam		
6 medium oranges		
1 ton of coal		
1 litre of 4-star petrol		
1 litre of emulsion paint		
pair of best-quality shoes for a small child		
medium-priced men's shirt		
colour TV licence		
school meal		
prescription at chemists		
Totals		

Money and Banks

Have you ever been into a bank? How much money must you have before you can open an account of your own? Are banks only for rich people? If you have never had anything to do with banks, then a lot of the information on the next few pages may surprise you. Perhaps you will decide to open an account of your own this very day. There is no reason why you should not do so.

In Unit 1.8 you will find some information on money and how it works, and all about putting that money into the hands of a bank.

Before you begin looking at the material, consider what one clever man had to say about money. Francis Bacon wrote:

Money is like muck, not good except it be spread.

Money is not new. The first coins we know of were used 2,700 years ago.

The story of money begins before the days of notes or coins when simple bartering or swapping was used. One man raised chickens, another went hunting; at the end of the day they exchanged meat for eggs. That exchange was simple, but supposing you had lived in those days and wanted a new roof on your cottage? The thatcher says he will do the job for two cows, but you only keep sheep, so you have to find another farmer who will swap two cows for some sheep. It was all very cumbersome.

Money was developed to overcome all these difficulties, because everything could be measured in terms of the same thing—money.

When you buy a pair of shoes, pay the milkman, tender your bus fare, or put a coin into a cigarette machine, you are using money as a **means of exchange.**

Money must be:

Easy to carry	**Easy to recognise**
Hard wearing	**Easily divisible**
Able to maintain its value	**Hard to forge**

Lots of things are used as money: gold and silver, jewellery, precious stones, ivory and even cowrie shells. Most money acquires its value either through scarcity value or through common use. Diamonds and gold are scarce and therefore very valuable, but what makes our fifty pence piece worth 50p? The answer is common usage. Anyone will happily give you goods in exchange for your 50p coin.

By the Middle Ages, gold was the main currency in Britain, and the problem was how to protect it. At first people left their gold with their local goldsmiths because they had vaults to lock it away. Naturally the goldsmith made a charge for this service, and it quickly became a profitable side-line. The goldsmith gave a receipt for the gold stored away in his vault. These receipts began to be used as money and were handed from person to person in settlement of debts. These receipts were the beginning of paper money.

By 1709 the Bank of England was in charge of issuing banknotes, and up until 1931 it was possible to walk into a bank and exchange them for real gold.

What is written on a banknote? Look and see.

Today there are four big banks whose branches you will find in almost every High Street. They are:

The Midland Bank
The National Westminster Bank
Barclays Bank
Lloyds Bank

Other banks, like Williams & Glyn's, Coutts & Co. and the Co-operative Bank have branches in some places.

These days many ordinary people have a bank account and do their business through the bank. There are several reasons for this. For instance, it is difficult to deal with all your money needs in cash. You may well have bills which can most easily be paid by post. You may be saving your money and it is not safe to leave it lying around the house. Your employer may pay you by cheque. All these are reasons for having a bank account.

There are two basic kinds of **bank account**:

   i) A current account
  ii) A deposit account

A **deposit account** is for your savings. It will earn interest for you (for more about interest, see page 38), but you will receive a paying-in book not a cheque book.

A **current account**, sometimes called a cheque account, is the most widely used one. It enables you to put money in the bank and withdraw it by writing a cheque. This cheque is payable to yourself if you want cash, and to someone else if you want to pay a bill.

You only have to have £1 to open a bank account, though the bank will want to know a little bit about you and assure themselves that you are trustworthy.

Cheques and bank cards

Writing a cheque is simple, but it must be done carefully. There are five sections to be filled in on every cheque:

   i) The date
   ii) The name of the person to be paid
   iii) The sum of money in numbers
   iv) The sum of money in writing
   v) Your signature

At your own branch you can draw out as much money as your account will stand. Providing you have a **bank card** (supplied by your own branch) you can go into any branch of any major bank anywhere and draw up to £50.

Most shops will accept a cheque for up to £50 providing you have a bank card too.

Some bank cards are also **credit cards** (for example, Access and Barclaycard) and it is possible to use them without writing a cheque.

Some of the big banks also produce a **service card**. The service machines are outside the banks, and enable holders to draw cash, order a cheque book, or obtain an account statement even when the bank is closed.

The banks offer many other services too, including:
Travellers cheques are a safe way of taking your money abroad.
Standing orders are a way of letting your bank pay your bills for you every month.
Investment. The banks will help you to invest your money safely.
Loans. The banks are always happy to lend you money providing they feel you can be trusted with it and will be able to pay it back quite quickly.
Safe custody. The bank will look after your valuables for you.

Investing Your Money

Few of us have the sort of fortunes that enable us to just pop out and buy whatever we fancy whenever we fancy it. The big items, like motorbikes and cars, stereos and colour televisions, holidays and jewellery can only be bought after a period of careful saving.

There are still people who keep those savings in a 'safe' secret place in their home. Those people are very stupid. In the first place, burglars are very clever at finding those secret places—after all, they make a living at it! Secondly, if that money were put into some sort of savings scheme, it would be growing bigger. For example, if you had hidden £100 under your mattress a year ago today, then, burglars permitting, you still have £100 there today. If you had put that £100 into a savings plan a year ago, it could now be worth £110.

In Unit 1.9 we are going to consider two different kinds of saving, building societies, and the Post Office.

Building Societies

The aim of building societies is to collect money from people who wish to save with them, and lend the money to people who wish to buy a home. They are **mutual institutions**, which means they do NOT make a profit. The borrowers pay **interest** on the money they are borrowing; the lenders are paid slightly lower interest for the money they are lending. The difference is used to pay taxes and the cost of running the society.

Interest is the money a borrower (e.g. a building society) pays to the lender (e.g. you) on a regular basis. It is usually quoted as an annual rate; thus a rate of 10% per annum means that on a loan of £100, *at least* £10 is payable to the lender each year. It may be more, though, if the interest is **compound**. Let's look at an example.

Suppose a borrower of £100 undertakes to pay interest every six months. If the annual rate is 10%, for half a year it must be half of that, or 5%. So £5 is added to the original £100.

At the end of the year another 5% is payable. But it isn't calculated on £100, but on £105 (the original £100 + the £5 interest paid earlier). So the lender ends up with £110.25, not just £110. (If the interest were calculated *monthly*, the increase would be even greater. Nice if you are lending, as you are when you are investing; not so nice if you are borrowing, as for example in a hire-purchase agreement. Always find out exactly what you are *actually* going to pay in interest; it may be more than it seems at first.)

Building societies handle a great deal of business. In 1983 they held 40 million savings accounts worth £80,000,000,000. Many people choose to save this way because it is easy. There are branches in the High Street, the interest paid is quite high and there are no income tax complications.

The actual interest payable varies from time to time, but it is usually quite good (allowing for tax) compared with other kinds of investment; it also varies a little depending on the amount you invest, and the time you are prepared to leave it with the society. Check what the current rates are. (Note that the basic rate tax on the interest due has already been paid, so only if you have a high income will you pay any more tax.)

In 1869 the Building Societies Association (BSA) was founded, and almost all building societies belong to it. The Association lays down strict financial standards which all must follow, and in this way makes sure your money is very safe.

The Post Office

The Post Office advises us that we are never too young to start saving. For this reason they offer us a wide variety of ways of saving and investing our money.

Post Offices are open for longer business hours than the banks, and they also open on a Saturday morning, which is very convenient for working people. Saving with Post Office National Savings is very simple and straightforward.

Here are the five best known schemes they offer:

Ordinary Account

You only need £1 to start a Post Office Book (more properly called a National Savings Bank Ordinary Account). Once you are seven years old, you can put money in and take it out by yourself. While your money is in your account it earns you 6% (3% on small balances), the first £70 per annum free of income tax. You can pay in as little as £1 and up to £10,000. You can withdraw up to £50 at a Post Office counter; up to £100 by surrender of your book for checking; £250 if you have a Regular Customer Account; a larger amount with a few days' notice. With an Ordinary Account you can pay some bills up to £250 without handling cash, and can meet regular bills by means of 'standing orders'.

39

Investment Account

This method of saving is usually used for larger sums of money invested for a longer time. The minimum deposit is £1, and if you wish to withdraw your money, you must give the Post Office one month's notice. You do this by filling in a form. Money deposited in an investment account earns a favourable rate of interest and up to £200,000 can be put into this account. Interest varies, but the Post Office tries to keep it competitive with banks, etc.; it is taxable.

National Savings Certificates

These provide tax-free interest; some certificates are 'index-linked'—that is, they are adjusted in value to take account of cost-of-living changes. The interest rates and conditions vary according to the 'issue'—you should enquire at your local Post Office.

Premium Bonds

These are a very popular way of investing small sums of money. The minimum number you can buy is five £1 bonds. The method of paying interest is very different from other savings schemes. Instead of it being divided up between all the bond holders in relation to the number of bonds they hold, numbers are drawn at random by a computer (ERNIE) and the lucky people receive prizes. Every month bond holders have the chance of winning from £50 to £250,000 with every bond they hold. The disadvantage is, of course, that the odds are you will not win, and although you can always get your money back by selling the bonds, with inflation the £1 buys less and less each year.

National Savings—Save As You Earn

SAYE is a National Savings scheme whereby you agree to make 60 regular monthly payments into an account for five years. You can save between £4 and £50 per month, though once you have decided, it remains the same for the whole five years. The sum of money you get back at the end of five years will be your savings plus a sum of interest linked to the rise in the cost of living. If you chose to leave your money in the account for a further two years, you are paid an extra bonus. All interest is tax free.

Buying a House

Have you ever thought about buying a home of your own? It is an exciting idea, and it is quite likely you will make that decision within the next ten years. Many young people do not want either to share a house with their parents or in-laws or spend a lifetime paying rent on a house which will never be theirs.

Buying a house is the biggest purchase most of us make in a lifetime, and so we have to go about it very carefully. Over the page you will find a list of ten steps you have to take between deciding to buy your own and actually moving in. However, those ten steps are not in the correct order. Read the list carefully, and put them in the order you think appropriate.

Page 43 gives a summary of the basic financial factors involved in finding a home.

The second exercise on page 44 looks like a foreign language. It is, in fact, just the sort of advertisement that appears daily in our newspapers. Can you sort out what it means?

The final pages in this chapter give some basic information on mortgages—what they are, how they work, and how they vary.

IF YOU WERE BUYING A HOUSE IN WHICH ORDER WOULD YOU PUT THE FOLLOWING?

A   Look in the local papers for house advertisements and put yourself on the books of an Estate Agent.

B   Go to a solicitor and ask him to draw up conveyance documents and arrange dates for exchange of contract and completion of contract.

C   Decide how much you can afford each month for mortgage re-payments, insurance and rates.

D   Talk to Building Society/Bank/Town Hall for terms they would be prepared to offer on mortgage.

E   Decide whether you wish to buy old or new property.

F   Decide how much deposit you can raise.

G   Go to Building Society/Bank/Town Hall to make arrangements for mortgage.

H   Find a house you fancy, make the owner an offer, and shake hands on it.

I   Decide which area you would like to live in with reference to transport for work, shopping, etc.

J   Collect keys for your new house.

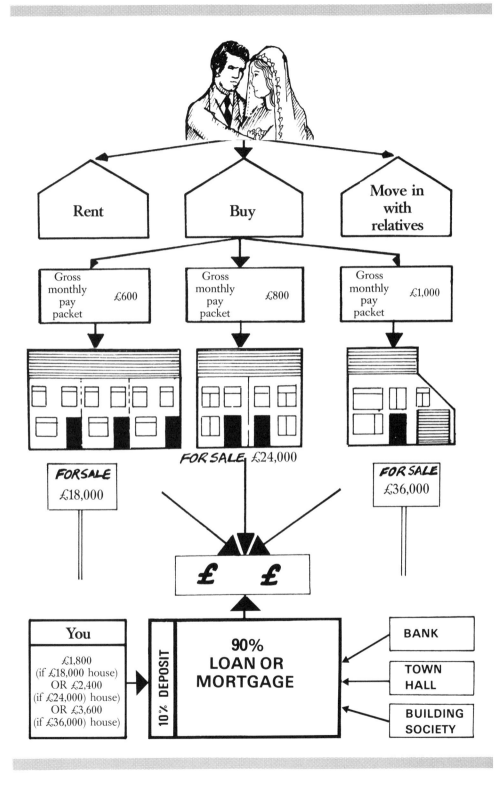

Rent

Buy

Move in with relatives

Gross monthly pay packet £600

Gross monthly pay packet £800

Gross monthly pay packet £1,000

FOR SALE £24,000

FOR SALE £18,000

FOR SALE £36,000

£ £

You
£1,800 (if £18,000 house) OR £2,400 (if £24,000) house) OR £3,600 (if £36,000 house)

10% DEPOSIT

90% LOAN OR MORTGAGE

BANK

TOWN HALL

BUILDING SOCIETY

What does the following Estate Agent's jargon mean?

dining room, kitchen, two bedrooms (one with shower off) Outside w.c. Gardens with possibility of car standing space at front. Viewing evenings and weekends

£21,500.

FERS BAS

OFFER BASED

HIGHLY DESIRABLE
PROPERTY
GUILDFORD AREA

G.floor. Porch, lg. hall, cloaks WC WB, 3 rec.—din.rm. + liv.rm. + lounge 25 x 20, study, fully fit. kit., ut.rm.

1st.floor. 2 sin.beds., 3 d.beds 1 with e.s.bath., add. bath., sh.rm., fitted robes each bed., balcony. Oil c.h. and d.g. throughout. Patio drs. to acre est.gdn.

D.garage. Easy walk shops, sch., stn. £82,000 ono.

View b.a. Akton & Arkwright, Guild.70832/3.

R BASED

OFFER BASED

FFER BASED ON £13,950

An ... residen... Centre and ... spacious accommodation comprises ... lounge diner, kitchen, three good bedrooms bathroom and integral garage. Neatly arranged gardens Ideal first purchase. Fitted carpets included Viewing Any reasonable time or through Agents

£28,750.

An attractive modern end mews house pleasantly situated in a popular residential area on the north side of Worcester convenient for to the link road and into the city centre The well laid out accommodation briefly comprises Porch reception hall lounge dining area well fitted kitchen three good bedrooms bathroom with ... Partially ... garage Garden Fitted ...

Mortgages

A mortgage is a loan of money against the security of a building. The lender of the money (THE MORTGAGEE) keeps the TITLE DEEDS (certificate of ownership) of the building, and has the right to sell if the borrower (THE MORTGAGOR) defaults on repayments.

Mortgage Deed

This sets out the rules and conditions of the mortgage, such as:
How the payments will be made.
How the mortgage can be ended by either the lender or borrower.
The interest calculations.
Insuring the home.
Altering the home.
Keeping the home in good repair.
Not letting the home.

Types of Mortgages

There are two main types of mortgage: repayment mortgages, and endowment mortgages. With a repayment mortgage, the mortgagee a) works out the total interest which is payable on the capital (the sum borrowed); b) adds this total interest to the capital; and c) divides the result by the number of months the mortgage lasts. (So, if the mortgage lasts 20 years, they divide by 20 x 12, or 240.) You then pay off some of the capital, plus some of the interest, every month.

With an endowment mortgage, you don't pay back the original loan (the capital) until the end of the mortgage; to make sure it *can* be paid back then (or earlier if you were to die), you take out an assurance policy. So, every month, you are paying a) some of the total interest on the loan, and b) an assurance premium.

Overall, your monthly payments with the two types of mortgage may not be very different. With many endowment mortgages, the assurance policy may give you more money at the end of the mortgage than you need to pay off the loan. On the other hand, you may be paying a little more each month with such a mortgage; really, what you are doing is to take out an extra life assurance policy as well as a mortgage. You have to decide whether this is worthwhile for you.

All building societies (and other people, like banks, who offer mortgages) will provide you with fuller details. Below, as an example, we show what you might pay monthly on a repayment mortgage. (Note that taxpayers at the standard rate don't pay tax on the interest part of mortgage repayments, and the table below takes account of this; it shows what you *actually* pay, after tax allowances have been made.)

LENGTH OF LOAN	Monthly payment per £1,000 borrowed, if standard tax rate 30%, and current interest rate is:					
	8%	10%	12%	14%	15%	16%
15 years	8.40	9.20	10.00	10.90	11.30	11.80
20 years	7.10	7.90	8.80	9.70	10.20	10.60
25 years	6.30	7.20	8.10	9.10	9.60	10.10

It is important to remember that after you take out the mortgage, the interest rate (and therefore your monthly payments) may go up. This is true for *both* types of mortgage.

Chapter 2

A Place in the Community

UNIT 2.1

Coming to Grips with Self

The following conversation took place between two friends walking down a street. One had just bought a newspaper from a bad-tempered paper boy.

'Does he always treat you so rudely?'
'Yes, unfortunately he does.'
'And are you always so polite and friendly to him?'
'Yes, I am.'
'Why are you so nice to him when he is so unfriendly to you?'
'Because I don't want him to decide how I'm going to act.'

Do other people decide the way you behave and think? This is what we are going to think about in Unit 2.1: ourselves and other people. The first thing we would like you to do is to interview, and be interviewed by, someone else in your group. See how much you can find out about them, and let them find out about you in just a few minutes. You will find some suggested questions on the next page. Following that you will find some more ideas to think about.

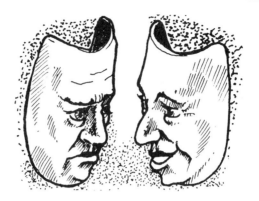

WHICH MASK ARE YOU WEARING TODAY?

Find out as much as you can about the person sitting next to you, so that in three minutes you will be able to describe him/her to others.

Find out

Name
Age
Where he/she lives
How he/she felt about coming on this course
What he/she likes doing
What he/she hates
If he/she is shy
If he/she has a sense of humour
What makes him/her laugh
What he/she does on Saturday nights
If he/she liked school
If he/she has a job
What he/she would like to do for a living
If he/she has travelled abroad
In what ways he/she is different from you
If he/she gets on with the family
etc.

Sugar and Spice and All Things Nice

Slugs and Snails and Puppy Dogs' Tails

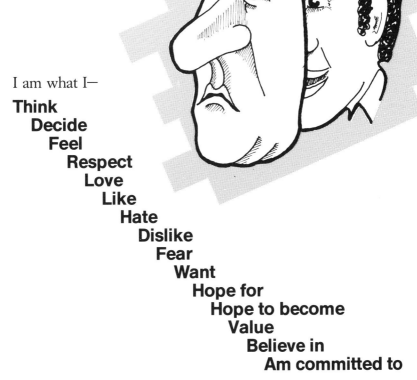

I am what I—

Think
  Decide
    Feel
      Respect
     Love
      Like
        Hate
         Dislike
        Fear
         Want
           Hope for
             Hope to become
            Value
             Believe in
               Am committed to

But if I tell you who I am, you may not like me, and I am all that I possess.

SELF-IMAGE QUESTIONS

Here is a list of personality characteristics. Tick the ones you honestly feel apply to you.

easy to get on with	easily worried
bad-tempered	selfish
reliable	affectionate
careless	jealous
self-confident	moody
generous	nervous
warm-hearted	bossy
considerate of others	shy
snobbish	sulky
sarcastic	outspoken
adventurous	helpful
honest	friendly
hard-working	quiet
excitable	quick-tempered
full of fun	gentle

Which is your worst characteristic?

Which is your best characteristic?

What characteristic do you most hate in other people?

Which characteristics in other people most attract you to them?

Make a list of characteristics you think a boy/girl would look for before he/she went out with you.

EVERY TOM, DICK AND HARRY

Below are some quotations from a number of people about relation-ships. What do they mean to you?

The person that each of us is, —is unique. (Piaget)

The main thing is not to be afraid to be human. (Pablo Casals)

Unless you love someone, nothing else makes sense. (e e cummings)

. . . those pathetic people who simply want friends and can never make any. (C. S. Lewis)

Love is important because if people did not love each other, there wouldn't be any people. (Seven-year-old girl)

To understand people, I must try to hear what they will never be able to say. (John Powell)

You couldn't make everyone in the world love each other. They don't even get on in blocks of flats. (Seven-year-old boy)

To live fully we must learn to use *things and* love *people, and not* love *things and* use *people.* (John Powell)

It costs so much to be a full human being that there are very few who have the courage to pay the price. (Morris West)

UNIT 2.2

Family and Marriage

Are you going to get married and have a family? It may surprise you to know that statistics prove that most of you will do just that within the next five years. How well will you cope with the responsibilities?

In Unit 2.2 we are going to consider this subject. Have a look at the two different kinds of marriage service on pages 56-57 and page 58. Then discuss the questions at the bottom of page 55. Finally, we go on to consider families and the homes they live in.

Out with the 'I' and in with the 'We'

The family unit has existed, in some form or other, down the ages in all civilisations and societies.

What does it really mean to live with another person—to break away from your existing family unit and form a new one? Are sex and security the only reasons, the main reasons, or just part of the picture? Does it need a legal document to bring people together, or can mature, adult people establish a meaningful relationship and live together with no ties? How long should these partnerships be for? Should a marriage licence be renewable after a period of time? If the formal family unit were abolished, who would look after, house, feed and clothe the vast number of dependants? The Church says marriages are for life, but can it ever be right to make people go on living together when they have grown to hate each other? Do you think broken homes have an effect on the children of the marriage? Is it better for two people who dislike each other to stay together for the sake of the children, or would the children be happier with just one happy parent?

There are many difficult questions for you to consider here, but they are questions to ask yourself before and not after you go into partnership with someone of the opposite sex. **Getting married is cheap and easy. Being married is costly and very hard work.**

GETTING HITCHED

What qualities would you look for in the perfect partner?

Why do you think men get married? Or women?

Would you choose a religious ceremony, or a civil one?

Do you think marriage is on the way out, or here for keeps?

What is the greatest advantage of $\Big\}$ living together?
What is the greatest disadvantage of

People say 'he chased her until she caught him'. What does that mean, and do you agree with it?

What would our society be like if there were no marriage?

A Church Marriage Service

There are several forms of Marriage Service.
This is one.

We have come together in the presence of God to witness the marriage of this man and this woman, and to pray for them. Marriage is a gift of God to mankind. Holy Scripture compares it to the Union of Christ with his Church. It should therefore be held in honour by all mankind. It must not be entered upon lightly or thoughtlessly, but responsibly and reverently. God calls men and women to the married state so that their love may be made holy in life-long union; that they may bring up their children to grow in grace and learn to love Him; and that they may honour, help and comfort one another both in prosperity and adversity.

If any of you is aware of any just impediment to this marriage, you are to declare it now.

I require and charge you both, in the presence of God, that, if either of you knows any reason why, according to the law of the Church or of this land, you may not be joined together in marriage, you now make it known.

The Lord be with you.
And also with you.

Almighty God,
   to you all hearts are open
   all desires known:
Purify our thoughts through your Holy Spirit
   that we may love you with heart and mind
   and praise you as we ought:
Through Jesus Christ our Lord. Amen.

BIBLE READING
PSALM
BIBLE READING

NAME will you have NAME to be your wife/husband? Will you live with her/him in obedience to God's will and purpose? Will you love her/him, honour her/him, and care for her/him in sickness and in health? Will you be faithful to her/him, and her/him alone, as long as you both shall live?
I will.

I, NAME, take you, NAME, to be my wife/husband,
To have and to hold,
From this day forward,
For better, for worse,
For richer, for poorer,
In sickness and in health,
To love and to cherish,
As long as we both shall live,
According to the will and purpose of God.
And to this I give you my pledge.

Bless, O Lord, this ring (these rings) given and received as a sign of
love and faithfulness. Amen.

Receive this ring as a sign of love and faithfulness between us.
I honour you with my body,
And all my possessions I share with you.

As NAME and NAME have consented together in marriage, and have
made their pledge to one another before God and this congregation,
and have declared it by joining of hands, and by giving and receiving of
a ring, I declare that they are now husband and wife. In the name of the
Father, and of the Son, and of the Holy Spirit. Amen.

Those whom God has joined together, let no man put asunder.

God the Father, God the Son, God the Holy Spirit, bless, preserve and
keep you; the Lord mercifully with his favour look upon you; and so fill
you with all spiritual benediction and grace, that you may so live together in this life, that in the world to come you may have everlasting
life. Amen.

PRAYERS

OPTIONAL COMMUNION SERVICE

A Civil Wedding

FORM OF MARRIAGE
(Bride and Bridegroom stand)

This place in which you are now met has been duly sanctioned according to law for the celebration of marriages.

Before you are joined in matrimony I have to remind you of the solemn and binding character of the vows you are about to make. Marriage according to the law of this country is the union of one man with one woman, voluntarily entered into for life, to the exclusion of all others.

Will you ... take ... to be your lawful wedded wife? (Answer—I will')

Will you ... take ... to be your lawful wedded husband? Answer— 'I will')

I do solemnly declare that I know not of any lawful impediment why I ... may not be joined in matrimony to ...

(Witnesses and guests stand)

I call upon these persons here present to witness that I ... do take thee ... to be my lawful wedded wife/husband.

(Ring is placed on third finger of Bride's left hand)

I give thee this ring as a token that I have taken thee to be my wife.

And now it gives me great pleasure to tell you that by virtue of the vows you have made to each other, you are now husband and wife.

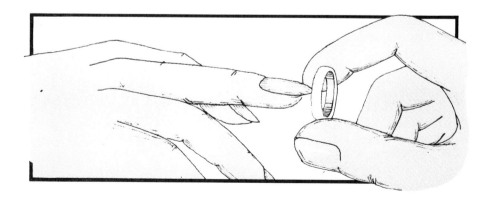

YOU AND YOUR FAMILY

Where you can, answer the following questions. Nobody but you will see your answers.

1. How important is your family to you?

   a) The most important thing in your life   d) Quite important
   b) Very important   e) Unimportant
   c) Important

2. To which member of your family do you feel closest?
3. Which member of your family has had the greatest influence on your life?
4. How would you describe your parents' relationship with each other?

   a) Very close   d) Cool
   b) Close   e) Distant
   c) Average

5. How many brothers and sisters have you?
6. Are you jealous of any of them?
7. Are you able to communicate with your parents?
8. Which member of your family would you choose to talk to if you were in real trouble?
9. Which of the following words (tick several) could you apply to your feelings for your parents?
   LOVE TRUST RESPECT LIKE HONOUR HATE DISTRUST DISLIKE IRRITATION
10. Do you think the family unit is altered if a grandparent lives in the house?
11. How often do you do things as a family?

    a) Constantly   d) Seldom
    b) Often   e) Never
    c) Occasionally

    Would you like to be able to answer that question differently?

12. Do you have family holidays?
13. What is the major source of arguments in your family?
14. Do you see yourself getting married and having a family?
15. Do you think your relationship with your children will be different from your parents' relationship with you? In what way?

A HOME OR ONLY A HOUSE?

These days an architect attempts to decide exactly what sort of needs the family has before he designs a house. He asks questions like 'Should there be one large living room or two smaller ones?', 'Where do most families like to eat their meals?'.

Below is the outline of the ground floor of a house. Divide it up into the rooms you think would make an ideal home for an average family.

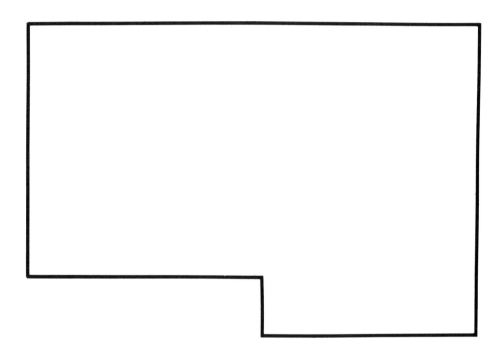

UNIT 2.3

Meeting Strangers

Have you ever interviewed total strangers? That is what you are going to try in Unit 2.3. On the next page you will find a list of questions on watching television. We would like you to go off in pairs for an hour, out into the street, and stop passers-by to ask them the questions. Be very polite. Explain where (and what) you are studying, and that you need to collect information. Try to interview a variety of people. Leave room on your questionnaire to tick their answers. At the end of an hour, return to your group.

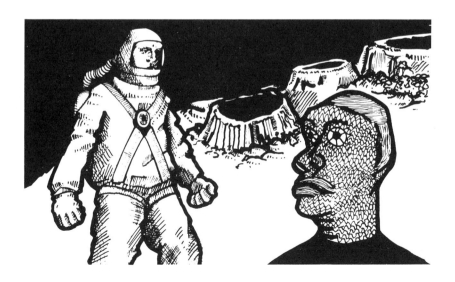

Questionnaire for the general public on television

1. Approximately how much television do you watch each day?
   None   **1 hour**   **3 hours**   **6 hours**   **+6 hours**

2. Which channel do you watch most?
   BBC1   **BBC2**   **ITV**   **Channel 4**

3. Do you watch television in the afternoons?
   Never   **Sometimes**   **Often**

4. How do you rate television news presentation?
   Poor   **Adequate**   **Good**

5. Do you think too much sport is shown on television?
   Yes   **No**

CONFRONTATION

We all react in different ways to different people and different situations. No one behaves in exactly the same way with his father, his boss and his friend. How would you react if suddenly brought face to face with the person in each of these pictures?

The Role of Women in our Society

This century has seen a great change in the life of women, and this is the subject we are going to consider in Unit 2.4.

On the following pages you will find a lot of questions which need careful thought. You are also asked to consider the work you think men and women should do. You might like to start by considering this quotation from an American comedian.

I make all the big decisions in our family, and my wife makes all the small decisions. She decides where we are going to live, what we will eat and wear, where the children go to school, how we spend our money and our weekends, and where we will go for our holidays. I decide who is going to be the next President, how the country should be run, if the Russians should build an 'N' bomb . . .

All are equal, but some are more equal than others

IS IT TRUE:

1. That men are bold and strong and make good protectors, while women are delicate and timid and need protection?

2. That men are born to command and women to obey?

3. That women make terrible bosses?

4. That men are more courageous than women?

5. That our children are paying dearly for the recent liberation of women?

6. That a woman's only true place is in the home?

WHOSE WORLD IS IT ANYWAY?

How would you feel if:

1. Your mother were the major wage earner in your family, while your father ran the house, looked after the family, and had a part-time job to make a little extra money?

2. Britain had not only a woman Prime Minister, but also a woman Chancellor of the Exchequer, a woman Home Secretary, and a woman Foreign Secretary?

3. It became the custom for women to go out to the pub for a drink in the evening (or the match on a Saturday) while the men stayed home?

4. All doctors were women?

5. One marriage partner was obliged by law to hand over all his/her wages to the other?

The Big Switch

CAN THERE BE EQUALITY?

In the space below each heading list:

The jobs that men cannot do	The jobs that women cannot do

Who decides this? Can old ideas be changed? Would the list be the same if we all lived in Russia or China?

UNIT
2.5

Prejudice

Prejudice is a funny thing; no one will admit to it, but we all think other people are prejudiced. What do you think of the following opinion of young people?

They all look alike these days, boys and girls, in frayed jeans and flowery shirts with patches on them. Their long flowing, dirty locks are probably crawling with lice, because it never occurs to their tiny brains to wash. They earn about £50 a week which is wasted on records and motorcycles, and they are completely promiscuous in their dealings with the opposite sex. They take drugs all the time and have no respect for their parents.

In Unit 2.5 we are going to consider prejudice of a different sort, colour prejudice and racial prejudice. There are three exercises for you to look at, all looking at these problems.

THE QUALITIES OF NATIONALITIES

Take one nationality at a time and put a tick by all of the characteristics you think apply to that nationality.

	American	French	German	Israeli	Italian	Jamaican	Japanese	Pakistani	Russian	English	Irish	Scottish	Welsh
1. Boastful													
2. Dirty													
3. Drunken													
4. Generous													
5. Good-tempered													
6. Hard-working													
7. Intelligent													
8. Lazy													
9. Polite													
10. Shy													
11. Sportsmanlike													
12. War-loving													

Your tutor will tell you how to score after you have finished.

The scoring is given in Tutor's Edition p. xvii

IS IT TRUE?

Answer YES or NO to each of the following questions. Be honest.

1. Is it true that more people now come into our country than leave?

2. Is it true that coloured immigrants have caused a housing shortage?

3. Is it true that segregation of coloured and white people has almost solved the racial problems in South Africa?

4. Is it true that anyone in Britain who is in need can get Family Allowance?

5. Is it true that if children of different races go to the same school they will not develop racial prejudice?

6. Is it true that eight per cent of Britain's population is Jewish?

7. Is it true that only 1.5 million of our population of 55 million are coloured?

8. Is it true that ten per cent of Britain's hospital doctors are foreign?

9. Is it true that while the average white family has 2.5 children, the average coloured family has five?

10. Is it true that negroes are more likely to commit crimes than white people?

The answers are given on page 70.

ANSWERS

1. No. 25,000 more people leave Britain each year than enter.
2. No.
3. No.
4. No. There is a three-year residential requirement.
5. Sadly no.
6. No. The figure is 0.8 per cent.
7. Yes.
8. No. The figure is 30 per cent.
9. No. The figure is 3.5 and this is going down.
10. No. Exactly the same.

How would you feel if one of these applied to you?

My son is marrying a foreigner.

My firm is sending me to live and work in Paris for a year.

I am a West Indian doctor and I have just bought a house in a street where everyone else is white.

I woke up this morning and found that my skin had changed colour.

I went for an interview for an apprenticeship yesterday, and they gave the job to a foreign boy.

UNIT 2.6

Fear

Are you easily frightened? Do you always avoid situations where you will 'stick out'? Do you watch the late-night horror films on television?

In Unit 2.6 we deal with two kinds of fear. First there is a list of common fears for you to tick. Second there are some questions we would like the whole group to think about.

THE FACE OF THE BOGEY-MAN

How frightened are you of the following common fears? Be honest and tick the appropriate column below.

	Not frightened	Frightened	Terrified
The dark			
Big dogs			
Confined spaces			
Getting lost			
Spiders			
Heights			
Flying			
Fire			
Suffocation			
Crowds of people			
Being alone			
Bees and wasps			

Please turn over now.

THE FACE OF THE BOGEY-MAN

How to gauge your results

Score 0 for ticks in column one
Score 5 for ticks in column two
Score 10 for ticks in column three

How many did you score out of a possible 120 marks?
If your score was either very high or very low, were you being entirely honest?

ARE YOU FEARFUL OF OTHER PEOPLE?

1. Does your heart race when you have to say something in front of other people? Do you think that people who have to make speeches all the time get over that fear?

2. Do you welcome big changes in your life, or are you frightened of them? How did you feel on your first day on this course?

3. Can you remember a situation you have been in when you were surrounded by others, but felt afraid? Would you have admitted that fear? Do you think others felt the same as you?

4. Do you think that everyone is afraid of something? Do you know anyone you could describe as fearless?

5. Do you let other people get 'close' enough to you to understand how you really feel? Can you tell when a friend is frightened or unhappy?

6. Why do you think people are so afraid of making fools of themselves?

Health and Fitness

In television advertisements for a 'super new vitamin pill' would you be featured as the 'Before' or the 'After'? In other words, are you the perfect example of vibrant good health, or a knobbly-kneed weakling with a permanent cold?

Many doctors are convinced that diet, sleep and exercise are the ingredients of good health, so on page 77 in this unit there is a questionnaire on your life-style.

On page 78 you will find some claims made by recent television and magazine advertisements. The product varies, but all contain an element of the 'health fetish'.

HOW TIRED DO YOU GET?

How many hours is your working day? _____

How long is your lunch hour? _____

What time do you get home? _____

How much time do you spend each day on travelling? _____

In your opinion which is more tiring, school or a job? _____

Which is more physically tiring? _____

How many hours of sleep do you think you need? _____

Do you feel more tired at the beginning or end of the day? _____

Do you feel tired when you are bored? _____

Do you think there is any connection between not eating sensible meals and feeling tired? _____

Do you feel more tired after a big meal or if you have skipped a meal?

_____

Do you eat **breakfast?** _____ **lunch?** _____

cooked tea? _____ **cooked supper?** _____

If you have to make your own meal do you:

    not bother? _____
    buy fish and chips? _____
    make a snack? _____
    cook a proper meal? _____

When you are tired, are you: **bed-tempered?** _____ **dozy?** _____

inclined to be silly? _____ **exactly as normal?** _____

In how many hours of sport a week did you participate

    three years ago? _____ **and now?** _____

Advertising

Consider the claims made by the following advertisements and try to decide the strength of their appeal, and how honest they are.

The Blackcurrant drink with extra vitamin C.

The growing-up spread for you, your children and your children's children.

The first person to test our golf shoes wasn't a British Open Champion. He was a doctor.

Your beauty is safe with us. Dermo-testing. Absolute purity.

Our new deep action conditioner with its protein formula works to make every single hair more beautiful, because in today's world your hair is constantly under attack.

Wake up. Here comes the sunshine breakfast.

Isn't nature delicious? Our founder was a Victorian authority on nutrition. He simply cleaned the wheat and ground it between two stones. We are doing the same today.

We don't tamper with the milk we use for our cream, yoghurt and cottage cheese. You see we think that nature should do most of the work, because that way we keep as much of the goodness of our natural products as possible.

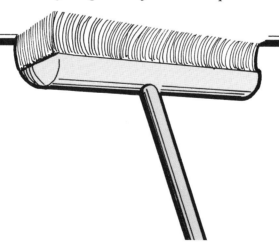

UNIT
2.8

Drugs

Do you know anything about drugs? Have you ever been offered drugs?
Could you become a drug addict?

Today the illegal drug scene is a very, very big problem. David Wilkerson, who runs an organisation called Teen Challenge, in New York,
helping drug addicts, writes:

*My parish is the gutter, and you won't find any children living in it. There
are only people, big ones and little ones.*

He means that drugs make old men and women of the youngsters who
depend upon them. And this is not just the problem of New York. You
can find junkies wandering round scruffy downtown areas of our cities
any night of the week.

THE ABC OF DRUG SLANG

Do you know what these mean?

Acid
Amps
Bar
Coke
Cold turkey
Connection
Downers
Fixing
Gear
Grass
Goofballs
H
Habit
Hash
Hooked
Horse

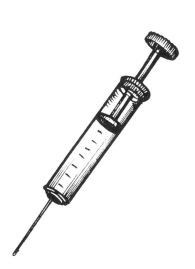

Jacking
Joint
Joy popping
Junkie
M
Mainline
Marijuana
On a trip
Opiates
PHI
Purple hearts
Script
Snow
Speed
Uppers
Weed

Below you will find some details

The world of illegal drugs has a jargon all of its own. The drugs themselves are frequently referred to as GEAR, and the supplier is known as a CONNECTION. A person under the influence of drugs is BLOCKED or ON A TRIP. When heroin is injected under the skin it is called JOY POPPING, but when the addict or JUNKIE injects heroin into a vein it is known as FIXING, JACKING or MAINLINING, and that is the most serious form of addiction. Why people become drug addicts is a frightening question, because addiction to hard drugs, the OPIATES, can only lead to death. One way of trying to break the habit (KICK IT) is by taking ever smaller quantities to wean yourself off drugs. Doctors will help addicts in this way by giving them prescriptions (SCRIPTS) for legal drugs. The other way to come off drugs is to go into hospital, come off the drugs very suddenly, and have expert help in coping with the ghastly withdrawal problems. This is called COLD TURKEY.

Why do you think drug takers have invented their own language?

80

Drugs fall into six main categories. Here is some information about them.

Opiates *Opium, heroin, morphine. (H, horse, phi)* These are the hard drugs which cause the most serious addiction. They are a sedative, or soothing pain killer. They make you feel good.

Cocaine *(Coke, goofballs, snow)* This is a stimulant and pain killer, once used as an anæsthetic especially by dentists. It is usually sniffed, and it makes you feel excited.

Amphetamines *(Amps, pep pills, uppers)* These are antidepressant pills often prescribed by doctors for people who are very depressed, and sometimes as aids to slimming. They make you feel elated.

Barbiturates *(Barbs, downers, purple hearts)* These are strong sedatives usually prescribed by doctors as sleeping pills. When combined with alcohol, they destroy your judgement of size and distance.

LSD *(Acid)* This is an hallucinogenic drug which can be used to great effect by psychiatrists. It revives memories and brings vivid hallucinations (mental pictures, day dreams). It is addictive and can cause permanent mental damage.

Cannabis *(Indian hemp, marijuana, hashish, hash, pot, joint, M, weed)* This drug is a sedative which is usually smoked. It makes you feel drowsy and happy and at peace with the world.

All these drugs are addictive—either **physically** (your body comes to depend on them) or **psychologically** (you feel you can't do without them).

Do you take drugs or do they take you?

WHERE NOW?

1. Why do so many drug addicts become criminals?

2. Why do we regard alcohol, nicotine (cigarettes, etc.) and caffeine (coffee, tea, chocolate, cola drinks) as acceptable?

3. What would happen to you if you took a) 1, b) 3, c) 10, d) 50 barbiturate pills?

4. What do you do to cheer yourself up?

5. There are 300,000 alcoholics in Britain today. What sort of people are they, do you think?

6. Do you find drunkenness funny? Why is it so often part of a comedian's repertoire?

Unwanted Pregnancies

Unwanted pregnancies are a fact of life; a problem with which individuals and our society are faced.

If you are like the vast majority of British people, you will have never really considered the issues involved in single-parent families, adoption, hastily arranged marriages or prematurely terminated pregnancies (abortions).

In Unit 2.9 you are asked to lift the 'blind' you have put down over your mind and really think about this subject. You will find some of the material shocking, but then so are many aspects of life. Perhaps at the end of the day you will still hold exactly the same opinions, but at least you will have considered the alternatives.

Abortion

The following material is put out by anti-abortion campaigners.
How do you feel about it?

Just a Blob of Jelly

When is a baby not a baby? Is a baby a person only after it is born, or sometime before? Does the following information surprise you?

At 25 days after conception the baby's heart is beating.
At 30 days the baby has a brain, eyes, ears, mouth, kidneys, liver and a heart pumping blood it has made itself.
At 45 days, about the time the mother is sure she is pregnant, the baby's skeleton is complete and it moves.
At 63 days the baby can grasp with its hands, is responsive to pain and touch and cold, wakes and sleeps, gets hiccups and sucks its thumb.

And 63 days is only nine weeks
Babies are aborted up to twenty weeks

How is an abortion carried out? There are three methods commonly used in our hospitals.
An injection A concentrated salt solution is injected into the mother, and the fœtus is pickled alive.
D and C Up to 12 weeks it is possible to scrape the fœtus off the wall of the womb and remove the bits by vacuum. One is left with a jar of blood with recognisable bits of baby floating in it.
Hysterotomy After 12 weeks and up to 20 weeks, the womb is cut open and the fœtus removed alive. The baby is perfect right down to nails and eyelashes. It will go on kicking for a long time and can take four hours to die.

Most people would agree that there are some instances when an abortion is necessary. For example, it is common practice when a pregnant woman catches German Measles. But does the information you have just read affect the way you feel about abortions? It does not prevent a lot of women from choosing to have them. Here are the figures for numbers of abortions in Britain.

1966 6,000	1971 125,000	1977 133,000
1967 Abortion Act	1973 167,000	1980 163,000
1969 59,000	1975 127,000	

Some hospitals now have more abortions than normal births, despite the fact that medical evidence seems to show that quite a few women having abortions (one in five has been claimed) suffer some permanent damage.

The whole business of abortion understandably makes a lot of people very emotional (some nurses won't take part in it). Almost everyone can agree that it's better to avoid making an unwanted baby in the first place. But what if there *is* a baby on the way? Certainly it is a big responsibility to end a potential life (some people would say a life already) in the womb. But isn't it perhaps an equally big responsibility to bring into the world an unwanted child, or a child who is so handicapped that any real understanding or enjoyment of life would be impossible? Those who support abortion would say that is not a very fair thing to do to a human being.

What do you think? On the rest of this page, and the next, we give you some questions to think about, and some cases to consider.

WHAT IF?

How would you feel *about abortion if* you *were . . .*
The unmarried mother-to-be?
The father of your girlfriend's expected baby?
The parent of the pregnant girl?
The doctor who had to perform the abortion?
The nurse who had to watch the operation?
The young married couple next-door who are unable to have children?
The unborn baby?

LIFE-OR-DEATH QUESTIONS

1. Do physically and mentally defective people have a right to life?

2. Is abortion the long-stop for contraception—an acceptable means of birth control?

3. Should a pregnant woman who is seeking an abortion be told all the details of the operation?

4. Under what circumstances would *you* be in favour of an abortion?

5. Assuming you are unmarried, how would an unwanted pregnancy (of yourself or your girlfriend) affect your job and career prospects?

CASE STUDIES

What do you think would be the right course of action in the following cases?

Jane is 13½ years old. She's an attractive, bright girl. Her parents are very proud of her, and especially proud of her ambition to become a teacher. At present, Jane is just home from hospital. She was there because something horrifying happened to her. She was walking home from a friend's house one evening seven weeks ago, when two youths stopped their car beside her and pulled her inside. Once they were clear of the town, they stopped the car, dragged her out, assaulted her and raped her. A passing motorist found her wandering along the road sometime later.

Jane is still too badly shocked to be able to talk about it. Her parents told their close family and the head teacher at her school, but the police helped them to keep her name out of the newspapers, and friends think she had a slight car accident. Now it is realised that Jane is pregnant.

Janet and Jerry are very happily married. Jerry works in a bank and they have a nice house on the new estate. They were very happy to discover that Janet was pregnant; so were the four prospective grandparents. Now doctors have warned them that it is almost certain that the baby will be born with a serious mental defect.

Jenny has always been a wild, irresponsible girl. Even when she was still at school, no one seemed to be able to control her wild temper and viciousness. She hasn't been able to hold down any sort of job. Her parents worried themselves silly when she began to hang around the dockland pubs, and it didn't surprise anyone when she 'got herself pregnant'.

Jean is twenty years old, and married to Jack who is the same age. Things have been very difficult for them recently. Jack lost his job when the factory closed down, and they lost their home with Jack's mother when she decided to go and live with her sister 200 miles away. They have a nine-month-old baby, and it is very cramped in their bedsitter—though it is all they can do to pay for that. Now they have discovered that Jean is pregnant again.

Violence

Violence is a fact of life. It is not a phenomenon of this century; you only have to look through the pages of a history book to see that mankind has always been violent.

Some people say it is the law of the jungle—kill or be killed. Others suggest that we are instinctively violent for our own survival. A third thought is that violence is infectious—we learn to be violent because we live in a violent world.

In Unit 2.10 we consider the question of violence from a number of angles. Are you violent and aggressive? Fill in the questionnaire on the following page and see how your total compares with others in the group. Look at the slogans printed on page 89. How much truth do you find in them? Why are men more violent than women? Consider the material following the slogans.

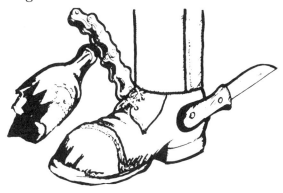

HOW AGGRESSIVE ARE YOU?

1. When you have quarrelled with someone, are you the first to apologise:
   a) **always?**
   b) **sometimes?**
   c) **never?**

2. Do the people who know you think of you as:
   a) **content and unambitious?**
   b) **easy to get along with?**
   c) **assertive and ambitious?**

3. Do you think of yourself as:
   a) **mild-mannered?**
   b) **self-confident?**
   c) **self-assertive?**

4. Do you lose your temper:
   a) **never?**
   b) **sometimes?**
   c) **often?**

5. Have you (since childhood) hit another person:
   a) **never?**
   b) **occasionally?**
   c) **often?**

6. If you were a motorist in a traffic jam, would you:
   a) **remain calm and collected?**
   b) **swear under your breath?**
   c) **lose your temper with other motorists?**

7. When something goes wrong, do you:
   a) **accept it as one of those things?**
   b) **get angry with yourself?**
   c) **blame others?**

8. If you found a small boy stealing apples from your tree, would you:
   a) **let him keep them?**
   b) **make him give back the apples?**
   c) **phone the police?**

9. If you are badly served in a shop, do you:
   a) **say nothing because you don't want to make a fuss?**
   b) **tell the assistant you are displeased?**
   c) **demand to see the manager?**

10. In politics would you describe yourself as:
    a) **disinterested?**
    b) **middle of the road?**
    c) **an extremist?**

Scoring

Now work out your scores. For every answer a) score 1 point, for b) score 5 points, for c) score 10 points.

If you have scored between 35 and 65 you are averagely aggressive, able to assert yourself, and reasonably self-confident. If you have scored much over 65, then you must be careful not to be over-aggressive, ruthless and inconsiderate of others. If you have a very low score this indicates lack of aggression and self-confidence, and perhaps it is time you realised your own value a little more.

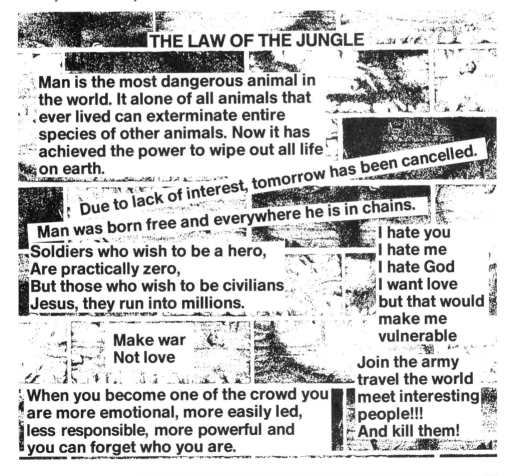

THE LAW OF THE JUNGLE

Man is the most dangerous animal in the world. It alone of all animals that ever lived can exterminate entire species of other animals. Now it has achieved the power to wipe out all life on earth.

Due to lack of interest, tomorrow has been cancelled.

Man was born free and everywhere he is in chains.

Soldiers who wish to be a hero,
Are practically zero,
But those who wish to be civilians
Jesus, they run into millions.

I hate you
I hate me
I hate God
I want love
but that would make me vulnerable

Make war
Not love

Join the army
travel the world
meet interesting people!!!
And kill them!

When you become one of the crowd you are more emotional, more easily led, less responsible, more powerful and you can forget who you are.

World War One—ten million dead
World War Two—fifty million dead
World War Three—everybody dead?

There are many cumbersome ways to kill a man:
you can make him carry a plank of wood
to the top of a hill and nail him to it. To do this
properly you require a crowd of people
wearing sandals, a cock that crows, a cloak
to dissect, a sponge, some vinegar and one
man to hammer the nails home.

Or you can take a length of steel,
shaped and chased in a traditional way,
and attempt to pierce the metal cage he wears.
But for this you need white horses,
English trees, men with bows and arrows,
at least two flags, a prince and a
castle to hold your banquet in.

Dispensing with nobility, you may, if the wind
allows, blow gas at him. But then you need
a mile of mud sliced through with ditches,
not to mention black boots, bomb craters,
more mud, a plague of rats, a dozen songs
and some round hats made of steel.

In an age of aeroplanes, you may fly
miles above your victim and dispose of him by
pressing one small switch. All you then
require is an ocean to separate you, two
systems of government, a nation's scientists,
several factories, a psychopath and
land that no one needs for several years.

These are, as I began, cumbersome ways
to kill a man. Simpler, direct, and much more neat
is to see that he is living somewhere in the middle
of the twentieth century, and leave him there.

Edwin Brock, from *Penguin Modern Poets 8*

> *Oh, damn! I know what I am;*
> *I'm a creature who moves in*
> *Predestined grooves.*
> *I'm not even a bus,*
> *I'm a tram.*

Little boys are expected to be
. . . able to control tears, dirty, allowed to swear, fighters, interested in guns, independent of their home, able to climb trees, good at playing cowboys, aggressive winners, tough, hard and inconsiderate.

Little girls are expected to be
. . . in need of comfort, often in tears, clean and tidy, never allowed to use bad language, non-fighters, fond of skipping and playing with dolls, frightened of leaving home, attracted to flowers, looking forward to having a baby of their own, able to lose gracefully, tender and affectionate, able to keep out of trouble.

In Britain 95% of all crimes of violence are committed by men.

Chapter 3

Becoming a Worker in the Community

The World of Work

Why do people work?

There are certain things that every person in the world needs in order
to stay alive: food, clothes and shelter. Without these we would die
quite quickly; therefore people work to provide for these basic needs,
because only by working can they be provided. If no one worked, no
one would survive. Of course, there are millions of people who don't
work yet survive quite well, e.g. pensioners, children, college students,
those too ill or incapacitated to work, and those who cannot find work.
All these people, however, are supported by those who work. They
could not be supported otherwise.

What is 'work'?

We have already said that we all have basic needs; fortunately for us nature provides all these needs for us: our food, clothes and materials for our shelter. All we people have to do is to

a) collect or move nature's provisions;

b) change, process or refine them for our benefit.

The first task is to move or collect natural materials, i.e. the wheat from fields, coal or oil from under ground. The second task is to change them into forms which are directly usable: flour, petrol, nylon and so on.

Not all work would fall into the categories mentioned; indeed in the more advanced countries of the world only a small percentage of people carry out work of this kind because there is a great demand for other services, e.g. doctors, teachers, policemen, footballers, entertainers. What is a fact, however, is that we all depend on others to a degree in order to live the sort of life we wish to live. To sustain our life, work must be done.

DISCUSSION POINTS

Compare the types of work British people do with the work done in the poorer countries of the world.

Compare the variety and types of food, clothes and shelters that are used throughout the world.

With more and more work being done by machines, will there come a time when all work will be done by machines and men will be redundant?

Role-playing

Now choose a job and explain why you think it is important.

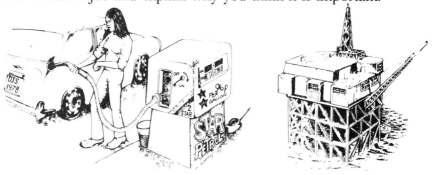

Why is work becoming more difficult to find?

Man has probably never really enjoyed hard physical work. He has always tried to find easier ways of doing things. You must have heard people say such things as, 'There must be an easier way of earning a living than this' or 'There must be easier ways of doing this task than this'. This desire to make it easier for himself—to take the effort out of the job—led him in due course to invent simple hand-tools and ultimately machines. Today these machines do the job for him. The early machine did the physical work of man; now our machines do the mental work as well.

The result of all this is that when firms, large or small, install machinery in their factories, it usually means that less effort is required of the workforce. In some cases, fewer people are required to operate them. *Man is making himself redundant.* Some people say that by the end of this century some 10 million jobs will disappear in this country. Should this occur, what would be the likely consequences? Would it be a good thing or a bad thing in your estimation? If those who *cannot* find work are well paid for *not* working, who do you think are the lucky ones—those working or those not working? Should we halt the progress of automation so that jobs are protected, or should we try to invent new jobs? What might those new jobs be? Would early retirement and shorter hours solve part of the problem?

As many of our jobs are dangerous, dirty, disease-causing and boring, perhaps it would be better if people did not work at these jobs, and let the machines get on with it. After all, machines don't have to worry about danger, dirt, disease or being bored.

Perhaps man is nearing attainment of what could be his greatest achievement—greater than the wheel, the computer or the silicon chip. That achievement would be living without having to work, because all needs would be taken care of by machines. If this could happen, what would be the implications? What would people do with their time? Who would decide who had what? Would there be any need for money?

UNIT
3.2

Job Choosing

What sort of a job am I looking for?

It is important to start asking yourself questions about the sort of work and job you want to do as soon as possible, because there are hundreds of different types of jobs in hundreds of different types of firms and organisations, all over the country. Although jobs are not easy to come by, there is still a wide range of possibilities. You should discover as much as you can about as many jobs as possible in order to give yourself a picture of what is most likely to suit you.

If you are exceptionally good at something such as playing football, playing a musical instrument, or painting pictures, the decision is probably an easy one. If you are as most people are, average in most things, you will need help and guidance in arriving at decisions. Your Careers Officer is highly qualified to help you make these difficult decisions.

Whoever you may go to for advice is likely to ask these fairly basic questions. What answers would you give?

What job(s) would you most like to do?

Are there any jobs you would not wish to do?

Do you wish to pursue a career or are you content to take anything that comes?

Do you want to further your education and become technically qualified?

How far are you prepared to travel to a job?

Are you prepared to live away from home?

The job you do will not only affect your standard of living, it is also likely to affect your attitudes to life and even your personality. Because you will spend such a large part of your conscious life in work, you should ask yourself what are the important qualities you wish to get from your work. Here are a few of the qualities which different people have asked for in their work. After you have read them, consider them carefully for a few minutes, and rank them in the order which you think is the most important.

a) **Prospects** Many people have ambitions to 'get on', to 'improve myself', as they say. If you are like this, you will want a job which will enable you to achieve the kind of promotion you desire. On the other hand, you may wish to stay in the same type of job all your working life.

b) **Hours of Work** Different jobs require people to work different hours; farmers will tell you they work to maximise the available daylight; builders often work as much time as they can when the weather is suitable. For most people there is a more ordered system; 7.30 a.m. to 3.30 p.m.; 8 a.m. to 4.30 p.m.; 9.00 a.m. to 5.00 p.m. five days a week. There are also the shift workers who might work from 6.00 a.m. to 2.00 p.m.; 2.00 p.m. to 10.00 p.m.; 10.00 p.m. to 6 a.m. for a few days at a time, or perhaps for a whole week on one shift. How would you like to work shifts? You would probably get more money for doing so, but your social life could be restricted when you work 'afternoon' or 'night' shift, or weekends.

c) **Conditions** Conditions at work vary greatly; some jobs have pleasant surroundings—warm, comfortable offices where you can wear good clothes. Other jobs are dirty and dangerous, requiring special clothing;

some people have to work outside in all winds and weathers. Remember too that 'white collar' workers can expect to live longer than 'blue collar' workers.

d) **Money** We all wish to be paid for our work, and the more the better. Can a well-paid job compensate for the possible danger or boredom? Could you think of a job that you would not do, no matter how well paid it is?

e) **Job Satisfaction** Everyone would wish to do interesting, satisfying work, but not everyone does. Many jobs are very routine, repetitive, even boring. In such jobs people frequently will avoid going to work for the faintest reason. Those who find job satisfaction in the work tend to lose less time than those who don't.

f) **Security** With so much unemployment and redundancy about today, many people feel that security is the most important quality to seek in a job. Certainly, the fear of a person losing his job can have a great effect on that person.

DISCUSSION POINTS

How did your ranking compare with others in your group?

Do you think that your ranking of these qualities would be the same were you married for five years with a child and a mortgage?

How would you expect a married man of 50, with his mortgage paid and his children married, to rank them?

Should you judge a job by the starting wage, or by what you think the job will offer in the future?

Is there any noticeable difference between the girls' ranking and the boys' ranking?

Girls, how would you rank these qualities for your husbands? If you were also working, would that affect the ranking for a) yourself, b) your husband?

Put them in your order of importance (1,2,3,4,5,6)

Prospects	_____
Hours of work	_____
Conditions	_____
Money	_____
Job satisfaction	_____
Security	_____

UNIT 3.3

Job Preferences

It goes without saying that people should look for jobs they will enjoy doing, or that they should avoid jobs which would drive them mad. However, many people do jobs for all kinds of reasons, and some of the reasons may be wrong ones—e.g. parents trying to get their son or daughter to be what *they* would like to have been. People sometimes want to do the same job as a friend, only to find they haven't the same interest or ability as the friend. *Can you think of other wrong reasons?*

By this time you may well be asking: how do I know what the job will be like until I try it? We can never say for certain which jobs will suit you best; what we would say is that careful consideration of certain factors can lead you in certain directions and/or away from others. Have a look at the two questions on page 102. They may tell you a lot about yourself.

1. WHAT DID I ENJOY AT SCHOOL?

What subjects were you best at? Which did you enjoy most? (Are your two answers the same?) Try to think of the subjects themselves rather than the people who taught them. Now write a few lines on *why* you think you enjoyed the subjects.

_____

_____

_____

_____

_____

_____

_____

_____

_____

2. WHAT DO I ENJOY DOING IN MY SPARE TIME?

Some of the things we do in our spare time could be a type of work, although we don't get paid for doing it. Do you enjoy painting and decorating your house, working on the family's car, gardening, dress-making, sport, cookery, playing a musical instrument, babysitting, help-ing others to make things, youth work . . . ? The list could go on for pages! Again, you may serve on committees; you may help to organise some activity with or for others. If you do any one of these activities and enjoy doing it, perhaps you could do it for a living—at least now you're thinking about it. Now write a few lines saying whether you think one of your interests could lead to a full-time job.

_____

_____

_____

_____

_____

_____

_____

_____

_____

Categories of jobs

Now that you have looked at yourself, let us have a look at jobs and see what we can find out. Jobs, like cars and music, tend to fall into broad categories. An obvious category would be *outdoor* jobs. Such jobs would include: farming and fishing, forestry, market gardening, construction work and surveying. Another category is *social* jobs. These jobs involve working *for* people rather than working *with* people, and people doing them include: teachers, nurses, child care workers, social welfare workers, nursery assistants. Another broad category is administration. These jobs are usually 'indoor' or 'office' jobs; they include: secretarial and clerical work, banking, accounting, and sales.

Perhaps you would like to do a *practical* job. Examples would include: fitting and turning, electrical and building, production, working as a line operator, sewing machine operator, or an operative in a factory.

The next category to mention is *medical*. Jobs in this category are fairly obvious—e.g. nurses, vets, physiotherapists, midwives, pharmacists and doctors.

Finally we could mention a very broad category where the work is of an *artistic* nature. People in this category include: artists, writers, journalists, musicians, potters, engravers, window dressers, and designers.

We have given only a few jobs in these categories but in fact there are scores, even hundreds. We would also point out that not all jobs fit comfortably into specific categories; some combine elements of two or more (did you notice nurses?) For example a vet is *medical* and *outdoor*, and many *practical* jobs also call for *artistic* talents, e.g. interior decorating.

What category or categories would your sort of job fit into?

Please give some thought to what you really would like to do. Don't just be content with anything! What do you really want from life, and what have you got to give to life? Remember: if our ancestors had been content with their lot, we would still be living in caves! One thing is certain: if you just wait for things to happen, or take the attitude that something will turn up, you may drift into a job which is not suitable for your particular skills. The people who do well at work and who enjoy their work are usually the ones who thought about it and who made things happen for themselves.

UNIT
3.4

Where to Look

Having got a fairly clear picture of the job you would like to do or the career you wish to pursue, the next step is to find it. There are a variety of places to look; here are a few of them:

The Careers Office
Employment Agencies
Jobcentres
Newspapers—local and national
Television advertisements
Trade journals

In addition to these you should also write to firms and organisations which might have suitable vacancies in the future. Your name will go on the list for consideration when such vacancies arise. You might also ask friends or relatives to enquire where they work for possible vacancies. Don't be afraid to turn over any stone in your quest; at times such as these, persistence is a virtue.

Reading Job Advertisements

You should know where to start looking for a job. In newspapers, Careers Offices, Jobcentres, etc., you will see jobs displayed as advertisements. We now want you to be aware of what to look for in these advertisements, as misunderstandings could be embarrassing and could jeopardise your chances of success. Here is a list of the usual items found in such advertisements.

Name of the firm or organisation

Location of vacancy

Nature of vacancy, i.e. job title, duties and responsibilities, conditions of work, wages, holidays

Qualities of applicant, i.e. age, experience, qualifications, other abilities

Date for last reply

Where to apply

To whom to apply

Look at the advertisements for jobs which follow and look for the points listed above.

BIRKENTOWN VALLEY DISTRICT COUNCIL
requires
RECORD CLERK
in COUNCIL OFFICES at BIRKENTOWN

Duties include keeping records of work done on council property, recording stores and spares used, and requisitioning replacements. $37\frac{1}{2}$ hour week Mon-Fri, four weeks annual holiday, contributory pension scheme. Successful applicant should be 16-18 years of age, have at least 4 C S E s including English and Maths.

Applications to Personnel Recruitment Officer, Birkentown Council Offices, Birkentown, not later than 11th June. Mark envelope BKT/RC1.

EXPERIENCED OPERATOR
required for

HEAVY PLANT
Must be prepared to travel.

Write or 'phone E. Thomas,
Tynecastle Plant Hire Ltd.,
Tynecastle. Tel: Tynecastle 4321

WANTED
YOUNG IMAGINATIVE
COOK/CHEF
Small country house in Devon.
Fresh ingredients, lots of scope.
Good wages. Live in.
Ring Uppercoombe 307
Ask for Higwell.

UNIT 3.6

Applying for a Job

There are a number of ways to apply for a job. The most common are: letters of application; application forms; telephoning. Which of these three would you prefer to use? It is just as well to look closely at all three methods to ensure you are competent with each.

Letters of Application

If you write for a job you must write a suitable letter; you should treat this letter very seriously because it is very important. Remember the following:

Use ink or ball-point pen—and not pencils, crayons or felt-tipped pens.

Write on good-quality paper—don't tear a piece of paper out of an old school exercise book. Buy a decent writing pad if necessary.

Write as neatly and clearly as possible. Be prepared to write your letter a number of times until you get it right.

Always check your letter afterwards to ensure there are no spelling mistakes. If you are in doubt, refer to a dictionary or get someone else to check the letter for you.

A Letter of Application should include:

1. Your address—so that the reader knows where to reply.
2. The reader's address—a necessary formality.
3. Date. Use 3rd February 1985, rather than 3-2-85 as numbers can be confused for a different date, i.e. March 2nd 1985.
4. The reason you are writing the letter, in your first sentence.
5. Your age.
6. Schools attended, giving dates.
7. Certificates, including subjects passed and grades.
8. Work experience, if any.
9. References or testimonials.
10. The final compliment should always match the opening greeting or salutation, e.g. If you begin your letter 'Dear Sir' or 'Dear Madam', you must end it 'Yours faithfully'. If you begin by using someone's name: 'Dear Mr. Jones', Dear Mrs Jones' or 'Dear Miss Jones', you must end it 'Yours sincerely'.

Other points to remember are:

a) Only use 'Dear Madam' if you know the reader is a woman, otherwise presume it is a man and use 'Dear Sir'.

b) When you sign your name it is automatically assumed you are male unless you write in brackets after your signature 'Miss', 'Mrs' or Ms'.

EXERCISE

Now write a letter of application, for the job you wish to do, to the organisation or firm for which you would most like to work.

Then compare it with the sample letter over the page.

A TYPICAL LETTER OF APPLICATION

> XYZ Commercials Ltd.,
> 41 Commercial Street,
> ANYTOWN.
>
> 12 High Street,
> HOMEVILLE,
> AB1 2CD.
> 3rd Febuary 1985
>
> Dear Sir,
>
> I wish to apply for the vacancy you have for a clerk, which was advertised in today's Daily Clarion.
>
> I am seventeen years of age and am at present working as a records clerk with DeLuxe Autos Ltd, Homeville, as part of the Youth Training Scheme, organised by the Manpower Services Commission. I shall complete my YTS programme on 22nd July.
>
> I attended Queen Street Comprehensive School from September 1979 until July 1984 and passed five subjects in the C.S.E. examination. They are: English, Mathematics, History, Geography and General Science, all at grade three.
>
> I am available for an interview at any time, and I can provide you with two references, should you wish to see them.
>
> Yours faithfully,
> A. B. Jones (Miss)

Remember this: a well-written letter is likely to get you an interview; a badly written letter is likely to prejudice your chances.

Completing Application Forms

Many firms or organisations, particularly the larger ones, request people to 'fill in' application forms rather than write letters. This is done so that these organisations get the information they want about the applicants.

Application forms are often quite complicated affairs: some can be very confusing, many are badly designed. However, it is no use complaining when you are faced with one; you just have to get on with it and make sure you do a good job of it. A badly completed application, like a badly written letter, can ruin your chances of success. Your ability to fill in the form will be taken to be a measure of your general ability. You should aim to complete it *without making any mistakes.*

We suggest that you do the following *before* you start to write:

1. Read through the application form a few times to make sure you know what you are being asked. If you are unsure or in any doubt as to what you should do, ask someone on whom you can rely for help.

2. Make a rough draft on another piece of paper—make your mistakes before you start!

3. As with the letter of application, use only blue or black ink or ballpoint pen. Never use a pencil, crayon or any other colour ink.

4. Write as clearly and neatly as possible. Be conscious of the layout of your writing so that it is attractive to look at.

5. Always check on completion for omissions or mistakes. Remember, a well written application form will get you an interview!

EXERCISE

Here is an application form for you to complete; take your time, remember all you have been told. You will be glad of this practice when you have to do it 'for real' in the future! When you have finished the form, your tutor will collect it and distribute it along with the others to the members of your group. The 'form' which someone else has completed and which you are now asked to assess, may have some mistakes or omissions. Critically examine it and see what sort of an impression it makes on you. Is it 'very good', 'not bad', 'poor'? Is it better than yours? If so, why? Can you see the effect your application form is likely to have on the reader, and why it is so important to make a good job of completing it?

Application for position of . . . .

Surname	Mr/Mrs/Miss	Address
Other Names		

Date of Birth	Place of Birth	Present Employer

Schools/Colleges attended (Give dates)		Examinations Passed (and grades)

Leisure Activities	Previous Employment

When would you be available to start work?

1st Referee _____

Name _____

Address _____
_____
_____

2nd Referee _____

Name _____

Address _____
_____
_____

Applying by Telephone

You may be asked to apply for a job by telephoning someone in a firm or organisation; such details will appear in the advertisement. This sometimes happens when the firm wants to know what you sound like and what your telephone technique is like, before they interview you. This requires different skills from those needed to write letters and complete application forms.

Again we have several points for you to remember. When telephoning it is more important to remember the points than when writing a letter, as you can rewrite a letter. You can't remake a telephone call which goes wrong!

Before you telephone

1. **Use a private phone if possible, rather than a public coin box phone.** A call-box can be awkward and embarrassing when you have to keep feeding it with money. If you have to use a coin-box, take plenty of money with you. It would be awful to run out of money in the middle of your conversation.

2. **Get all the essential information to hand before you make the call:**
   a) the number and extension
   b) name of person to speak to
   c) where you saw the advertisement
   d) schools and dates you attended
   e) examinations passed and grades
   f) whether you have previously worked, and if so for how long
   g) what courses you have been on at work and at school or college.

You may think it unnecessary to write down all these details for a telephone call, but be assured, it isn't! You are likely to be nervous, and nerves can play all kinds of tricks with your memory. You don't want to appear foolish, do you?

How to speak on a telephone

Speak slowly—without blatantly dragging your words.

Speak clearly.

Speak loudly enough—don't mumble.

Speak in your natural voice—don't try to be 'posh' or clever.

If you miss something which was said, ask for it to be repeated.

You should remember these points whenever you make a telephone call. The telephone is here to stay; now is the best time to learn to use it!

UNIT
3.7

The Interview

All you have done so far is to get yourself to this stage—the interview. If your application has been satisfactory, the firm or organisation will be interested in you and will want to learn more about you before they take the chance of employing you. After all, if you work for them for ten years, they will be paying you a fortune in wages. So they will want to be as sure as it is possible to be.

You, in turn, have shown an interest in them by applying, but you too will want to learn more about them; you want to see what they are like. This then is the purpose of an interview—for both parties to assess each other.

Selling Yourself

What to do before going to an interview

Remember, you want to impress them so that they will offer the job to you—after the interview you may not want it, but it is pleasant to be offered, even to refuse. We suggest you do the following:

a) Find out as much as you can about the firm.
1. What do they do, or make?
2. Who owns the firm?
3. When was the firm established?
4. How many work for them?
5. What facilities have they for their employees?
6. Are they good to work for?

The reason for knowing some or all of the above is that you are likely to be asked if you know anything about them during your interview. If you can 'trot out' these items, they will be most impressed.

b) Ensure that you know where you have to go and how to get there. It is disastrous to arrive late and say you could not find the place—this shows a lack of initiative and you will probably fail before you start. It is a useful tip to make the journey, if possible, a day or two before the interview to familiarise yourself with it. You will have enough to occupy your mind on the day without transport problems.

c) List all the points you want answered:
1. What training is given and how long does it last?
2. What prospects are offered?
3. Is further education offered?
4. Employee facilities, canteens, etc.
5. Pay and how it is calculated.
6. Holidays.
7. —add your own!

Most, if not all the above information will probably be told to you during the interview, but just in case, be prepared to ask about it.

d) Have your certificates, references and letter calling you to interview ready before you go. Don't start looking for them as you are about to leave your home.

e) What are you going to wear? Decide what clothes you will wear a few days before and make sure they are all clean and pressed. Look as clean, well-groomed and as tidy as you can. Don't overdo it; try to be as comfortable as you can.

When you arrive at the interview

Most places have a receptionist or an enquiry desk—report there telling them who you are and why you are there. Someone will then tell you what to do or take you to the room of your interview.

The interview

The interviewer will introduce himself or herself to you, and may introduce other members of the panel to you. Don't sit down until you have been invited to do so. Sit comfortably, don't be too stiff and don't slouch. Don't smoke and don't chew! Whoever is doing the talking, look at that person and show your are concentrating on what he/she is saying—react to his/her words.

You will of course be asked many questions. The way you answer will make all the difference now; try to remember the following:

a) Speak clearly.
b) Speak slowly.
c) Speak loudly enough for all to hear—usually people speak too quietly, especially girls.
d) Whoever has asked the question, look at him/her when answering and always look *at* them!
e) Give full answers. Don't just answer 'Yes' or 'No'; this doesn't tell the interviewer(s) very much about you. Avoid 'Yeah' or 'Aye' for 'Yes' or 'Nope' for 'No'.
f) Don't try to be clever or to speak in a way you don't usually speak—be natural.
g) Don't put your hand near your mouth; this affects your speech.

Opposite you will find some typical interview questions. Try to fill in some suitable answers.

TYPICAL INTERVIEW QUESTIONS

1. Why have you applied for this job? _____
   _____

2. Do you know anything about this firm? _____
   _____

3. What do you think is involved in this job? _____
   _____

4. Do you see yourself ever as a supervisor or foreman? _____
   _____

5. What advice have your parents given you? _____
   _____
   _____
   _____

6. What makes you think you are suited to this type of work? _____
   _____

7. What are your hobbies or interests? _____
   _____

8. What sort of things should a person be sacked for doing? _____
   _____

9. If you are asked to work shifts in the future would you be prepared to? _____
   _____

10. What personal qualities do you think you possess? _____
    _____
    _____

11. What career do you wish to pursue? _____
    _____

12. Would you prefer an extra half-day off a week, or extra pay for the
    current working week? _____
    _____

13. If you have an important date or engagement that evening, but you
    have been asked to work on to finish a very important job, what
    would you do? _____
    _____

14. Would you prefer to work unsupervised or with the supervisor in
    close contact? _____
    _____

15. What advantages are there in attending a college for further edu-
    cation? _____
    _____

Starting Work

When you start work, it means that someone wants your skill, strength, knowledge or several abilities to work for him; in return he is prepared to pay you for those abilities. This is a perfectly fair arrangement. Because you are being paid for what you are doing it means that you are, or will be, doing a valuable job of work in conjunction with others. As a result, work is a system of trust, if it is to work well; trust between employee and employer.

When you were in school, if you didn't do your work, the teacher may have been disappointed, sad, even angry, but it didn't make any difference to his livelihood. Again, if you didn't attend school, it only meant one student less in his class. Your school friends too were unaffected by your work, whether good or bad; they were unaffected by your absence except perhaps socially. Now that you are in work, whatever you do will affect everyone else. If your work is good and you are trustworthy and a good time-keeper, it makes it easier for everyone else. In fact you are likely to be well accepted. If the opposite is true, it makes it difficult for others and you could be disliked and unpopular.

Your change of status requires a conscious awareness of the attitude needed in work. Perhaps you would like to think about the questions on the following pages and discuss them with your colleagues in the group.

ATTITUDES TOWARDS YOUR BOSS

He has his job to worry about and he has more problems than you.

The boss is likely to have a boss who is continually chasing him for results.

The boss is probably doing a fairly good job, or he wouldn't be where he is.

If someone complains about the boss (or anyone else for that matter) don't necessarily accept it without question. Formulate your own opinions, speak as you find.

If you work for a large firm or organisation, your boss is only carrying out other people's rules and orders. Don't blame him for the firm's rules, he may have no more say in them than you.

'He who pays the piper calls the tune.' Do you agree?

Remember this: whatever his/her faults may be, any fool can make non-constructive criticism—in fact, most fools do!

WORKMATES

Workmates are rather like families; they are not chosen, they are just there. Like a family, a workforce works for the benefit of the firm and the mutual benefit of each member. What do you think are the qualities of a good workmate?

QUESTIONS FOR DISCUSSION

1. If you could see a way of saving your firm a lot of money, and which could be highly rewarding for you, would you suggest it, even though it would mean making a colleague redundant?

2. Because a colleague has been repeatedly arriving late for work, the boss has issued an ultimatum that the next time he is late he will be sacked. This particular morning he is late again; you see the boss on his rounds; you know he will ask where your colleague is. What will you do:
   a) say he is in but has gone to the toilet?
   b) say you don't know where he is?
   c) say he is late again?
   d) go to the toilet yourself to get out of the way?
   Discuss your decision.

3. You and your colleague operate a rather expensive piece of machinery. You have noticed of late that he has become very erratic and careless—so much so that he has nearly caused a few accidents. Also your output is falling and your bonuses are in jeopardy. From what he has said, from his general behaviour, and from knowing the group he goes round with, you suspect he is taking drugs. Do you:
   a) tell him your feelings and threaten to report him?
   b) have a word with the boss?
   c) mind your own business?
   d) seek advice from other colleagues?
   Discuss your decision.

4. Mike, 18, has been an apprentice in a garage for 18 months. For the first nine months he was a fairly average apprentice, quite satisfactory but nothing exceptional. He then joined a 'pop' group, playing bass guitar. The group had quite a few engagements, and it was noticeable that Mike was regularly arriving late for work and asking for time off to go with the group. After five months the boss told him that unless his attitude to work changed and his time-keeping improved he would have to take disciplinary measures. For the next four months Mike was a model apprentice. However, last weekend Mike asked the boss if he could have Saturday morning off as he wanted to go to a 'Pop Festival' with the group. The boss allowed him to go. The 'Pop Festival' was a great success and went on for longer than was scheduled. Mike, having travelled in the group van, didn't have enough money to catch a train home on the Sunday evening, so he stayed with the group who returned in the early hours of Monday morning. He didn't arrive home until 6.00 a.m., went to bed and slept till noon. He reported to work as usual on Tuesday.

What would you do if you were the boss?

What should Mike have done to help himself?

If the boss had sacked him, what would his chances be of getting a similar job?

Could his parents force Mike to give up the group?

What advice would you give Mike?

Your Employer's Obligations

Having looked at your attitudes and responsibilities to your employer, we now have to look at the responsibilities and obligations your employer has towards you. Although employers vary, the conditions of work in different places will vary, and rates of pay will vary, there are certain things that all employers must do, by law. On the following pages you will find some of the important ones and what they mean.

Contracts of Employment

Whoever you work for in a permanent capacity (regular employment rather than casual work) must give you in writing the terms of your employment. This is called a 'Contract of Employment'. Your employers must state the following:

a) Your full name
b) Your employer's name and address
c) What your job involves
d) The date you started working for them
e) Your hours of work each week
f) What you will be paid
g) When and how you will be paid
h) Your holiday entitlement
i) What you must do when ill
j) Details of any pension schemes
k) How much notice to quit you must give or receive when you leave
l) What happens if you or they have a complaint

The employer will draft the 'Contract' and must give you a copy to read within 13 weeks of starting your job. Either you will be given a copy to keep, or the contract will be located somewhere where you can read it when you want to.

Any change in the details of your contract must be recorded on the contract within a calendar month of the changes being made.

The Contract of Employment states how much notice you employer must give to you if your employment is being ended. These periods of notice vary from job to job, but by law they must not be *less* than the following:

Length of service	Notice necessary
Up to 1 month	None
1 month–2 years	1 week
Over 2 and under 3 years	2 weeks
Over 3 and under 4 years	3 weeks
—then one extra week per year up to:	
Over 11 and under 12 years	11 weeks
Anything over 12 years	12 weeks

The contract normally also states how much notice *you* must give if you want to leave the job. The legal minimum, if nothing is stated in your contract, is seven day's notice, if you have worked continuously for at least four weeks.

Other things to note

1. You cannot transfer your contract from one firm to another. You must have a new contract.

2. If your firm is taken over by another firm, your existing contract will still be effective.

3. If you don't have a contract within 13 weeks of starting work, you should speak to your employer. If this doesn't work, you should seek legal advice from your trade union, or Department of Employment Office.

Stoppages

Your employer is obliged to deduct certain monies from your pay—not for his benefit though, but for the government. These deductions (sometimes called stoppages) include:

Income Tax

Every wage earner must pay tax to the level stipulated by the government. Some people won't pay tax because their income is less than their personal allowance. These personal allowances are calculated by the Inland Revenue Department. If you have a taxable income then your employer will deduct the tax each week from your pay packet and send it to the Collector of Taxes for your area. The amount of tax you pay will be stated on your payslip.

For more information on tax, look back to Chapter One, Unit 1.5.

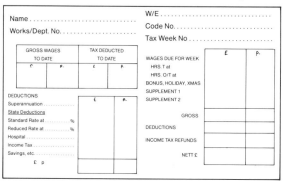

An example of a pay slip

National Insurance

This is a very special type of insurance which compensates people when they are unable to earn a living. Everyone who contributes for a sufficient period is entitled to claim benefits in time of need. Such benefits include:

a) Unemployment
b) Sickness
c) Disablement
d) Maternity benefit
e) Retirement pension
f) Widow's benefit
g) Widowed mother's benefit

Your contribution to this will be collected by your employer, and he too must pay a contribution for you to this scheme.

For more information on this and on the Department of Health and Social Security, look back to Chapter One, Unit 1.3, or contact the local office of DHSS.

Redundancy

One problem of work today is redundancy; each week it seems we hear of workers being made redundant. Redundancy doesn't just mean being sacked, it means that the job an employee is doing will cease to exist. However, people made redundant are normally entitled to compensation, if they have worked continuously for the organisation since the age of 18, for at least two years. (Working time *before* the age of 18 is not counted.) The following table shows how redundancy payment is calculated.

Age	Rate per Year of Employment
18–21	$\frac{1}{2}$ week's pay
22–40	1 week's pay
41–64 men 41–59 women }	$1\frac{1}{2}$ weeks' pay*

*For higher-paid employees, or those with very long service, there are some limits to the total amount of redundancy pay they can receive.

Note. As these ages, amounts and rates are constantly under review, they may have changed by the time you are reading them. Jobcentres or Careers Offices will give you the up-to-date details.

Trade Unions

A man once gave each of his five sons a stick and asked each son to break his stick; they did so with ease. He then took another five sticks, bound them tightly together, then gave the bundle to each son and asked each in turn to break the sticks. They could not break them.

This is the basic idea of trade unions. Individually people are not strong and can be broken; collectively or united there is a greater strength and fortitude.

When Britain became industrialised with many people working in factories, mills and mines, they had to endure much hardship and misery. They were 'slaves' to a very powerful system. Individually their attempts to change things were futile, so they began the long, often disappointing and violent movements for working people to gain recognition and expression.

From their early simple origins the trade unions of Britain have grown to be a major force in our land. Their activities are not merely confined to industrial matters, but are spread far into such areas as politics, social welfare, education and recreation to mention but a few. Some people feel that their influence is more than it should be, and that their activities should be curtailed or controlled by law. However, they can look back on a proud history of achievements for the raising of the living standards of the working man and woman. They have done much to bring about the changes in our society which we now take for granted as our rights.

The purposes and functions of a trade union are:

1. To negotiate on behalf of its members with the employers for improved pay, hours and conditions of work, and to decide what action to take should negotiations fail.
2. To defend the rights of each member.
3. To give legal assistance to its members.
4. To act as a 'friendly society' in providing social, recreational and educational facilities.
5. To establish political funds.
6. To discuss union matters with other unions both in this country and abroad.

Some of the activities of the trade unions

They have:
a) Allowed and enabled workers to express themselves
b) Maintained democracy and 'fair play'
c) Increased the status of the ordinary worker
d) Given workers confidence and a great sense of security
e) Become involved in national decisions
f) Become involved internationally

Some of the problems of trade unions

a) Demarcation disputes
b) Unofficial strikes
c) Gap between leaders and the rank and file
d) Lack of involvement by rank and file members (only five per cent attend meetings)
e) Influence from external pressure groups
f) Fewer than 50 per cent of workers are members of a union

DISCUSSION POINTS ON TRADE UNIONISM

Is it ever right to go on strike? If so, when?

Why do some groups of workers strike more frequently than others? (For example, car workers as opposed to shop workers.)

Should certain workers be denied the right to strike? (e.g. Police, Army, Nurses)

Should unions be allowed to align themselves to political parties?

Should the government get involved in union disputes?

Should individuals be obliged to join a union?

Can unions be too powerful?

What is 'secondary picketing'?

Should picketing be allowed?

A BIBLIOGRAPHY

Things That Matter Philip Grosset *Evans.*
But Deliver Us From Evil John Rickards *Darton, Longman and Todd.*
Rise of the Meritocracy Michael Young *Pelican.*
Brave New World Aldous Huxley *Penguin.*
Guide to the Social Services Family Welfare Ass. *Macdonald and Evans.*
Business Law S.B. Marsh and J. Soulsby *McGraw-Hill.*
Foreign Places Foreign Faces Jennifer Rogers *Penguin.*
Out of Your Mind Peter Newmark *Penguin.*
Money Sense in Society G. Studdard *Nat. Savings Comm.*
The Cross and the Switchblade David Wilkerson *Spire Books, USA.*
Just Off Chicken Street F. McLung *Revell Co., USA.*
Why I Am Afraid to Love, Why I Am Afraid to Tell You Who I Am
  J. Powell *Fontana.*
Adolescence Cyril Smith *Longmans.*
Unqualified, Untrained and Unemployed Nat. Youth Employment
  Council *HMSO.*
Connexions Colin Ward *Penguin*

ACKNOWLEDGEMENTS

Acknowledgements are due to: E. Brock and Secker & Warburg for permission to reproduce 'Five Ways to Kill a Man'; Church in Wales Publications for use of their Wedding Service.